JN023796

多文化理解のための
国際英語文化入門
Introduction to Studies of English Languages and Cultures

ウェルズ恵子 編

丸善出版

は じ め に

この本について

　本書は，英語を知的に使えるようになりたい人や，英語を使って学んだり研究したい人，自らの考察を英語で書き表したい初心者用の本です．といっても，英語の学習書ではありません．《国際英語文化》を知り，学びたい人が読者です．そのため本書は，日本語の導入文と英語による小論が組み合わさっています．「英語ってどういう言葉？」「日本語や私たちの文化との関係は？」「英語に関連して何が専門的に勉強できるの？」「英語の論文はどんなもの？」という好奇心に，本書は応えようとしています．義務教育で英語を学び終え英語で専門知識に触れ始める人，人文系の学問に興味があり英語を使って発信したいと望む人に役立つ本です．

　本書が示す《国際英語文化》とは，グローバルな共通語としての英語（国際英語）が生成する文化や，英語によって広まる文化を表します．世界中でそれぞれの土地と文化に応じた英語バリエーションが使われている現状を踏まえ，世界の英語および，そこから発生し発展していく文化の総体を国際英語文化としています．そして，《国際英語文化》を認識する前提として，「国際英語」ないしは「世界の英語」をどうとらえ，考察し，教育し，またそれを使って「何をどう研究するのか」について，最初の一歩を読者に示すことが本書の目的です．

グローバル・コミュニティへのチケットとしての英語

　私たちはさまざまな基準で共同体（コミュニティ）を構成し認識します．近くに住んでいれば地域共同体，同じ学校の卒業生なら同窓という共同体，親族という血縁共同体もあれば，同業種組合のような共同体もありますね．これらは物理的に把握しやすいものですが，目に見えにくい共同体もあります．文化すなわち「人のすること，感じること，考えること」の類似が人々をつなげます．趣味でつながるコミュニティがあり，政治信条で連帯する人々も共同体を成すことがあります．

　いずれの共同体においても，言語は人と人との結びつきに重要な役目を果たします．言葉遣いは世代や生活環境を表しますし，同じ趣味をもつ人々は分野の特殊語彙を共有しています．インターネットを使って頻繁に特定の情報を交換する人々は匿名のままに意思疎通する集団をなし，こうした共同体はインターネット・コミュニティまたはオンライン・コミュニティと呼ばれます．互いに「通じる」

言語を共有するとき，その人々は仲間となる第一段階をクリアしています．

　人類の活動範囲が地球規模に及ぶ現代，グローバルな言語として英語が使用されるようになりました．特定の一言語が世界で共通して使われる現象は，世界の人々が「地球で生きている仲間」なのだと認識するのに役立っています．英語というチケットを手に入れてグローバル・コミュニティに参加する，それが英語を学んで積極的に使う理由の１つです．

言語と社会，言葉と人

　社会と言語とには，深い繋がりがあります．社会を形作る文化の大きな部分は言語で成り立っています．私たちは言葉を使って知識を学び，愛を語り，異論を唱え，祈りを捧げます．そうした行為の１つずつが文化です．また，言葉を使ってより深く他人を理解し，自分を客体化し，世界の様子を認識し，歴史を綴ります．本書には，英語に関連した文化や英語の基盤となっている文化，英語で発信することが特に望まれる文化の例が紹介してあります．

　言語ないし高度なコミュニケーションツールは人を人たらしめるものであり，言語そのものが文化です．１つひとつの単語には人々の生活の歴史が潜んでおり，言葉の使われ方に共同体の特質や社会の問題が指摘できます．言葉のつくりは人間について深い洞察を提示し，言葉の教育にはアイデンティティに関わる思想が反映されます．その上，テクノロジーの発達や社会変動が人の生活を変えるのに伴い，新たな言葉の文化が続々と生まれます．本書が示すように，人と言葉は密接に関わり合っており，言語は常に変化する動的な性質をもっています．

この本の使い方

　何よりも，この本を楽しんでいただけたら，筆者はとても嬉しいです．こんな研究があるのか，面白そうだなと感じてくだされば，まずは目的達成です．その次は，読者自身が研究するときの参考書として使ってください．

　各章の日本語文は，研究分野や研究方法の紹介と研究素材の説明をしています．各章の筆者がその研究をどう楽しんでいるとか，どんな価値があって研究に取り組んでいるかが述べられています．英語文は，研究入門者向けの小論文の体裁になっています．ですから，読者が英語で論文を書くときの参考にしてください．英語文は各分野で論文を書くときの基本的な約束事にのっとって書かれていますので，スタイルを真似することもできます．引用の仕方や参考文献表の様式，英語論文で有用な語彙や専門用語などを学ぶことができます．章末には初心者向けの文献案内があります．また，【考えてみよう】は，読者が自分で研究を始めるときのヒントにしてください．

ウェルズ恵子

謝　辞

　言葉と文化と研究が楽しく関連し合い，グローバル視野の学際研究に読者を誘い込む本が作りたいと思ったのは，十数年も前のことです．でもそのときは，誰にどういう原稿をお願いしたらいいのか，また自分にまとめ役ができるのかもわからず，モヤモヤしながら何もせずに時を過ごしてしまいました．ですが，ようやく出版がかないました．もともと英語の勉強が大の苦手だった私が，英語に直接関係する本を出すなんて，笑ってしまいます．多くの方の協力があってのことです．感謝にたえません．

　本書の執筆と作成にあたっては，立命館大学文学部国際コミュニケーション学域の先生方の協力を得ました．英語教育・バイリンガル教育の第一人者で元同僚の湯川笑子さんから，研究者としてのみならず教師として英語に向き合うことを学ばせていただいた経験は，本書の実際的な出発点になっています．出版の基礎となった研究は，2021年度の立命館大学国際言語文化研究所・萌芽研究プログラムの援助を得て進めることができました．このときの研究チーム※が編集を後押ししてくれました．特に，チームメンバーの岡本広毅さんと杉村美奈さんには，原稿の整理を大いに助けていただきました．ユタ州立大学／コロラド大学出版社の元編集長で朋友のマイケル・スプーナー（Michael Spooner）さんからは，英語部分の編集について有用な助言をいただきました．これらの方々に，心より御礼申し上げます．

　加えて，立命館大学国際言語文化研究所・重点研究プログラム・ヴァナキュラー文化研究会（2020-2021年度）からも，研究資金の援助を受けました．出版にあたっては，同研究所より2022年度出版助成金を受けました．厚く御礼申し上げます．

　最後になりましたが，丸善出版の小林秀一郎さんには，拙書『多文化理解のためのアメリカ文化入門：社会・地域・伝承』（2017）に続いてお世話になりました．小林さんの励ましとご協力がなければ，本書は実現しませんでした．ありがとうございました．

　2022年8月1日

ウェルズ恵子

※　2021年度立命館大学国際言語文化研究所・萌芽研究プログラム研究チーム：岡本広毅（代表），杉村美奈，佐野愛子，薩摩真介，ウェルズ恵子

目　　次

国際共通語としての英語

Considerations on Teaching English as a Lingua Franca (ELF) in the Classroom

---

概要

今から 400 年ほど前，英語はほとんどイギリス諸島でしか使われていませんでした．しかし今では英語は世界中に広がり，その影響は様々な分野で活躍する何十億もの人々に及んでいます．本章では，今日の世界で英語がどのように使われているか，その使い方がどう変化し続けているかを説明します．加えて，国際共通語としての英語（ELF）の概念と，現在の ELF 研究を紹介します．最後に，21 世紀における英語の教育と学習について，アメリカ英語やイギリス英語といった伝統的なモデルではなく，ELF を重視すべきであることを論じます．一方，言語教室での ELF 教育に重点を置くことには，反対意見もあります．本章では最後にそうした反対意見を紹介します．

図1 「国際共通語としての英語」（**English as a Lingua Franca**）をめぐるキーワード［Adapted from ideas in Chapter 7 of *Introducing Global Englishes* by Galloway & Rose（2015）］

国際英語文化の中の ELF 研究

　世界中で広く学習されている英語は，標準的なアメリカ英語，標準的なイギリス英語です．しかしアメリカやイギリスでも，日常生活では多種類の英語のバリエーションが話されています．日本の公立学校では，日本からの生徒たちは標準アメリカ英語を学びます．一方アメリカを訪れてみると，生徒はこれまで学んできた教科書的な英語とは異なる言葉を話す人たちに出会うことになります．アクセントも違えば，日本の英語のテストでは間違いになるような文法を使う人もいて，驚くことでしょう．

　さらに視野を広げて世界に目を向けると，英語の種類はさらに増えます．大英帝国の植民地統治，それに続くアメリカの強大な経済力と文化力の影響によって，世界中に英語使用が広まり多様化しました．世界各国で話されている英語のバリエーションは，その国の人々の固有の言語や文化を反映しています．これらのバリエーションは，標準アメリカ英語や標準イギリス英語とは，文法，語彙，発音など多くの点で異なります．英語が話者にとっての母語であることもありますが，第二，第三の言語であることも少なくありません．そして，英語を非母語として話す人は，英語を母語とする人よりも圧倒的に多いのです．

　では，英語を母語としない 2 人が英語で会話するとき，その人たちはどのような種類の英語を使うのでしょうか．例えば，日本人とインド人が英語で会話する場合はどうでしょう．おそらくインド人は，自分が他のインド人に話す英語を少し調整し，インドの特有な語彙を避け，より普遍的に理解される語彙を使うでしょう．同じように，日本人はアクセントを調整したり，インド人にはなじみのない語彙を避けたりするかもしれません．言語学者たちは，このような妥協案を English as a Lingua Franca（国際共通語としての英語）（ELF）と呼んでいます．ELF 研究は言語学の中では比較的新しい分野ですが，世界のグローバル化が進み，文化的背景や母語の異なる人々が英語でコミュニケーションをとる機会が増えていることから，重要性が増しています．

　研究の視点は次のようなものです．ELF は「アメリカ英語」「イギリス英語」のような固定された種類ではなく文脈に依存していますが，言語学者が研究している ELF の種類には何か共通点があるのでしょうか．例えば，通常のテストでは間違いとされるような文法や発音の特徴はあるのか．もしあるなら，英語の学習者にそのような特徴を意識させたほうがよいのか，といったことです．そうすると，21 世紀の英語教育を考える上で ELF 研究には意義がありそうです．他方，現在の英語教育は，世界の英語の使われ方を反映していない古いものなのでしょうか．このように，グローバル化した世界で英語をどのように教えるべきかを考

える上で，ELF の研究は欠かせないものとなりつつあります．

研究の楽しさ

　ELF 研究は，グローバルイングリッシュの研究と密接な関係があります．この分野はとても魅力的で，世界中のさまざまな文化や言語を研究対象として包含しています．数年前まで，English「英語」という言葉は単数形の名詞としてしか使われていませんでした．しかし，世界中の英語が非常に多様性に富むことを言語学者が認識したため，現在では Englishes という複数形も使用されます．世界の英語を研究することで，私たちは世界のさまざまな文化について多くを学ぶことができます．

　有名な言語学者であるカチュルは，英語圏を 3 つの同心円に分けました．詳しくは後述しますが，①英語が母国語として話されている国，②英語が政府や教育，メディアの重要な言語となっている国，③日本のように主に他国の人々とのコミュニケーションのために英語を学んでいる国，です．第二グループの国々では，魅力的で豊かな英語のバリエーションが話されているのがわかっています．このグループには，インド，ナイジェリア，シンガポールなどの英語が含まれます．これらの国では英語が公用語の 1 つになっていますが，通常の生活で流通している英語は標準的な英語とはかなり異なります．最も顕著な違いは発音で，文法も私たちが考える標準的な英語とは異なるかもしれません．もう 1 つ重要な違いは，使用される単語やフレーズがこの人々の文化を強く反映している点です．イディオムの特徴は，異なる文化の知恵や価値観を知る上でとても興味深いものです．世界の英語の多様性と豊かさを理解すること自体が，ELF の研究を楽しく，教育的なものにしているのです．

この章のトピック

　本章では，ELF の現象をより詳しく考えていきます．まず，英語が世界中でどのように変化しているのか，また，異なる文化や言語環境にどのように適応しているのかを取り上げます．世界における英語の多様性と，ELF という考え方の登場について説明します．そして，ELF と英語教育の問題を取り上げます．

　グローバル化した現代においても，教えられている英語の種類は非常に限られることは明らかです．例えば日本では，公立学校の教科書には主にアメリカ英語が使われ，多くの学校で ALT（Assistant Language Teacher）を招いて授業

を手伝ってもらっています．そして ALT の多くはアメリカやイギリスなどから来た人たちです．これは，世界の英語使用の現状を十分に反映していると言えるでしょうか．ELF を意識した，もっと包括的な英語教育アプローチがあってもいいのではないでしょうか．その場合，学校で ELF を教えることにはどのようなメリットがあるのでしょうか．本章ではこうした重要な疑問を検討します．

　教室で伝統的な英語を教えることから脱却することへの批判も，本章は扱っています．ELF 教育は一部の生徒に不利益をもたらすのではないか．ELF が不定形な概念である場合，ELF を教えることは現実的なのか．ELF を教えても，学習者の利益という点ではそれほど大差はないのではないか．以上を検討した後，言語としての英語が世界中でどのように使用されているかという，より広い視野に立った将来の英語教育について考察し，結論を述べています．そして，伝統的な英語教育へのアプローチと，グローバル化した世界を受け入れるアプローチの両方の議論のバランスを取ることを提案しています．

研究の素材

　グローバルイングリッシュという分野は，言語学の中では比較的新しい分野であり，そのため，まだそれほど多くの文献があるわけではありません．このテーマに関する有名な書籍のいくつかは，本章の最後にある「その他の文献」のセクションで紹介しています．これらの本の中には，ELF の話題や教室でのその意味を扱ったものもあります．この章の内容の多くは，言語学分野における学術雑誌に掲載された研究論文に依拠しており，この分野に関心をもつ言語学者の研究に基づいています．同様に，教室での ELF の適用に対する批判は，言語学分野における雑誌の出版物に基づいています．そのような出版物の包括的なリストは「Further Reading」にあります．ELF とグローバルイングリッシュの分野をより深く理解するために，いくつかの有用なリソースが「Further Reading」で推奨されていますので，参考にしてください．

研究がめざすこと

　この研究の目的は，今日世界中で英語がどのように使われているかを理解し，それが英語教育にどのような影響を与えるべきかを考察することです．英語を母語としない人たちの交流は増えており，実際に日本人が中国人やインド人，その他の非英語母語話者と英語を使ってコミュニケーションをはかる必要性は大変に

高いという現実があります．したがって，現在の教室でアメリカやイギリスの標準的な英語を強調することが，グローバルなコミュニケーションツールとしての英語の教育という目的に合っているかどうかを評価し，調整する必要があります．さらに，現在の言語教育は言語の基本的な要素（文法，発音，語彙）に集中しすぎていて，グローバル化した世界で同様に重要な語用論的スキルや異文化間の相互理解に必要なスキルへの関心が不十分ではないのではないかと思われます．ELF 研究では，こうした問題の解決もめざしています．

Considerations on Teaching English as a Lingua Franca (ELF) in the Classroom[1]

TABLE OF CONTENTS

1. Introduction

The spread of the English language over the past four hundred years has put it in the unique position of being the world's first truly global language. A few years ago, the Indian linguist, Braj Kachru, tried to classify how English is used around the world. He designed a Three Circle model (cited in Galloway & Rose, 2015, pp. 17-18) and it has become one of the most common ways of explaining and categorizing the spread of English. It consists of three concentric circles: the *Inner Circle*, the *Outer Circle*, and the *Expanding Circle* as illustrated in Figure 1. The Inner Circle countries are those where English is the first language and, without doubt, the dominant language within its bor-

---

1 This chapter has been adapted from a paper written by the author entitled: *Considerations on the Use of Global Englishes in the EFL Classroom* published in the Ritsumeikan Studies in Language and Culture.

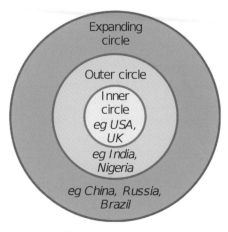

Figure 1   Braj Kachru's Three Circles of English [Acknowledgement: Awesomemeeos - Own work, CC-BY-SA 4.0, https://commons.wikimedia.org/w/index.php?curid = 60429594]

ders. These include countries such as the US, UK, and Australia. The Outer Circle countries include those where English plays an important role, often in government, business and education. Such countries tend to be former British colonies such as India, Ghana, and Nigeria. In many of these countries, English acts as a 'glue', a common language among a population with many different languages. In India, for example, although the Hindi language is spoken by over 40% of the population, they are mainly living in the northern and central areas of India. As a result, English is important as a language that can unite the whole country in many areas such as government, business, education, and the media. Finally, there are the Expanding Circle countries: These are countries where English has not played an important role, historically, but where it is taught in school and often used to communicate with people from different countries. Japan, China, Brazil and Russia are good examples of Expanding Circle countries. Many linguists now agree that the greatest area of growth in the use of the English language is between people from such countries. In other words, a growing number of interactions in the English language do not involve native speakers of English. Therefore, we must ask what effect this should have on the future teaching of English? This chapter will attempt to explain how English is changing around the world and how this could have repercussions for the teaching and learning of English.

2. How English is Changing around the World

Until now, the gold standard of English in classrooms around the world has been standard American English or standard British English. Curricula and examinations have mainly used these two varieties for teaching and examining students in their English proficiency. Indeed, to many people English still *belongs* to Inner Circle countries, but should we change our view of this? As American economic dominance in the world might decrease in the future, it may be the case that local varieties of English become more important. In recent years, more people have been thinking about the plural term: *global Englishes*. Seidlhofer (2004) states that " [English] is being shaped, in its international uses, at least as much by its non-native speakers as its native speakers" (p. 211). It is likely that English will continue its global dominance in the future, but which form of English people will be learning and speaking in the future is a matter of debate. What seems certain though is that English will be used more and more by non-native speakers in situations that do not include participants from Inner Circle countries.

3. Teaching English as a Lingua Franca (ELF)

In recent years there has been a growing interest in the use of English as a *lingua franca* (ELF). That is, as a form of English used by those who use English as a second or even third language. There have been suggestions that English language teaching should better reflect the current situation of English around the world. However, what do we actually mean by ELF? Samarin (as cited in Murray) defines a lingua franca as "any lingual medium of communication between people of different mother tongues, for whom it is a second language" (2012, p. 319). ELF is often considered to be what occurs when people, mainly from Expanding Circle countries, talk to one another. In other words, it mainly refers to communication in English between non-native speakers of English. However, it can also occur between "interlocutors from the Inner and Outer Circles" (Seidlhofer, 2004, p. 11). ELF is not seen as a *variety* of English such as American English, Indian English, and Nigerian English, as it is highly changeable depending on the backgrounds of those speaking it.

Some linguists, such as Jennifer Jenkins (2002), have even tried to make rules that can help in the English language classroom. Her Lingua Franca Core (LFC), for example, focuses on the core areas of phonology that are important for people to understand one another. The LFC therefore separates those areas of phonology which "need to be taught, and non-essential (non-core) items which do not" (MacKenzie, 2014, p. 124). Take the pronunciation of the 'th' sound in the words 'thanks' and 'this' which can vary even among Inner Circle varieties of English. There does not seem to be any problem in understanding the pronunciation of these sounds that differ from traditional standard varieties of English. Furthermore, Seidlhofer (2004) has added research to the concept of ELF in which she has identified some similarities in words and grammar that non-native speakers use. For example, the non-use of the 's' in the third-person present tense as in 'She play tennis'; not using articles such as *a, an,* and *the*; making plurals of uncountable nouns such as *informations* and *staffs* and so on. Such variations in English are thought of in Japanese classrooms as simply mistakes. Lesson plans and tests do not recognize these variations and try to promote a more *correct* Inner Circle standard of English. As Kubota (2018) points out, in the case of Japan, an Expanding Circle country, the clear majority of assistant language teachers employed in the government's JET (Japan Exchange and Teaching) Program are from Inner Circle countries—60% from the US alone. This is also reflected in the teaching materials, which have a high percentage of content based on the cultures and societies of Inner Circle countries. Therefore, from the start, students in Japan are exposed to native levels of English, which they can rarely hope to achieve, and they are tested on their accuracy in reproducing such native speaker levels. Kaur adds that "regardless of how ELF is used or what forms it takes, of fundamental importance is that its speakers achieve mutual understanding" (2010, p. 193).

4. Criticisms of Teaching English as a Lingua Franca (ELF)

However, there has been criticism of recognizing ELF as a teachable *variety* of English. According to Sung, there is a tendency for ELF researchers to "exaggerate the differences between ELF and English as a native language (ENL)" and it is not helpful to treat them differently (2013, p. 350). Therefore, perhaps it is too simplistic to separate Englishes in such a manner. Indeed, even within Inner Circle countries, there is a great variation in the dialects of English used. It is clear that English can no longer *belong* just to those people growing up in a traditional Inner Circle country. English has spread its wings and has been influenced by other cultures and languages for the past four centuries; this is a fact that cannot be ignored. However, to simply dismiss Inner Circle Englishes as irrelevant and inappropriate is to ignore their undoubted political and economic power. Sowden argues that offering an ELF curriculum would create schools with a two-tiered program: those schools where the more affluent students would choose to learn the native variety of English, and those where those who are not so affluent would have to choose the non-native ELF variety (2012). He predicts that such a separation would not just affect students, but teachers too. Those teachers who are native speakers of English would teach the ENL classes, while the other non-native speaking teachers would teach the ELF variety (2012). Sowden argues that such a policy might end up making the inequalities even worse.

Further to the criticism of ELF as a concept, let alone a variety that can be taught and learned, Swan points out that "many of the World English learners merely seek an effective working knowledge of the language, without wanting or needing a high level of accuracy" (2017, p. 513). To such learners, the availability of an ELF course would appear to be unnecessary. As long as their English didn't differ too much from the *standard* Englishes, then it wouldn't really make much difference. As Swan states, "[O] utside classrooms, it has always been taken for granted that NN [non-native] English varies, from near-native to something very different and that this does not necessarily matter" (2017, p. 511). Indeed, for all but the most competent learners, such differences in spoken English would be largely unnoticeable and unteachable.

5. Does Teaching and Learning English as a Lingua Franca Have a Future?

So, what does this mean for English language teachers and learners in the 21st century? Are teachers simply to continue with a standard American/British model of English, or perhaps introduce students to different varieties of English better suited to their needs in this globalised world? It is a difficult question and not helped by the fact that in many countries, Japan included, the demand for *authentic* varieties of English remains strong. In fact, throughout Japan, it is still mainly the case that language schools, as well as universities, prefer to employ native speakers of English rather than non-native speakers for most English language classes. However, as already mentioned, it is becoming clearer that *ownership* of English has expanded to include people who use it as a second or even third language. This reality has to be made clear to learners in order "to reflect his or her own sociolinguistic reality, rather than that of a usually distant native speaker" (Jenkins, 2006, p. 173). How far teachers can actually teach grammar forms that often appear in ELF is difficult to judge; after all, on a practical basis, common standards have to be set, taught, and maintained to keep everything fair.

It also seems that while ELF might be a rich area of research at present, it is mainly a phenomenon of spoken English. No one is suggesting that students should be reading or writing in such different ways. MacKenzie feels that the time has not yet come when we can present a model of English that lacks various forms such as the third person -s, countable/uncountable distinctions, irregular past forms and so on. Indeed, as he continues, " [l] earners will encounter all these forms in both written and spoken material emanating from inner circle countries" (MacKenzie, 2014, p. 167). Therefore, it is still important for students to be able to read and write a variety of English that is internationally acceptable so as not to put them at a disadvantage. Whether students use their English in business, travel, or education, the written form still conforms to native standard English varieties, and we cannot ignore this.

However, as research into ELF continues, it seems that opinions on how it can be used in the classroom have changed. Cogo argues that "there is ... an assumption that English Language Teaching (ELT) is all about grammar, vocabulary, and pronunciation and that is the sum of communication" (2011, p. 104). She continues by emphasizing that other areas of communication are equally important including communication strategies, as well as language and cultural awareness (p. 104). Therefore, in the globalized world of the 21st century, we need to move away from narrow definitions of English language teaching and better prepare students for global communication. Many English language textbooks still focus on native-speaker Inner Circle countries, their cultures, and their modes of communication. It is becoming more important for those who make such textbooks to include activities and content that more accurately reflect the reality of who uses English in the world today and how they use it. In the words of Kuo, these materials need "to raise consciousness of intercultural understanding" and to draw attention to "the fact that people from different cultural backgrounds tend to express politeness, gratitude, and condolences in overtly different ways" (2006, p. 19). This approach could be designed to suit the geographical location of students and provide what Murray describes as "a pragmatic 'toolkit' of strategies" to help them communicate with others in their region (2012, p. 324). Therefore, it is the responsibility of the teacher to decide which strategies best suit his or her students and introduce them alongside the traditional components of an English language program. It is also very important that textbook writers make more of an effort to address the realities of how English is used around the world today. This is not just with regards to providing communicative and pragmatic strategies, but also to give students opportunities to encounter Outer Circle as well as Inner Circle Englishes.

6. Conclusion

To conclude, the approach to teaching English has to become broader if it is to adequately prepare learners for coping in the globalised environment of the 21st century. Ownership of the English language has moved away from the traditional Inner Circle countries such as the US and UK, as more and more people around the world use English as a second or third language and use it with others who are also non-native speakers. We have termed the English that they use as *English as a lingua franca* (ELF). As we have discussed, it is probably unrealistic to teach a form of ELF to learners, as teachers would be teaching a spoken form of the language that differs from the written form and this could cause confusion. Apart from that, the expectation of students is still to be taught traditional standard models of English. Therefore, when we talk about ELF, we should not just focus on the traditional teaching of grammar, vocabulary, and pronunciation, but also include strategies and knowledge that will be of help to learners in communicative settings. To equip students with not only the linguistic skills, but also a *toolkit* to adapt such skills to various cultural environments, should be a necessary goal of English language classrooms. Of course, it will be difficult to overcome traditional attitudes toward teaching English in many parts of the world, where an emphasis on accuracy to pass examinations still persists. However, it is becoming obvious that such attitudes are old-fashioned and not suited to the way in which English is used around the world now. As Fang and Ren point out, "in today's globalized and multilingual world, ELT (English Language Teaching) practitioners need to be aware of the different needs and goals of students who will use English in different settings" (2018, p. 392). Therefore, it is very important that a greater awareness of how English is used in today's world and how to equip students to cope with it should be the aim of English language classrooms in the 21st century.

References

Cogo, A. (2011). English as a lingua franca: Concepts, use, and implications. *ELT Journal*, *66*(1), 97–105. doi:10.1093/let/ccr069.

Fang, G.F. & Ren, W. (2018). Developing students' awareness of global Englishes. *ELT Journal*, *72*(4), 384–394. doi: 10.1093/elt/ccy012.

Galloway, N. & Rose, H. (2015). *Introducing global Englishes*. Routledge.

Jenkins, J. (2006). Current Perspectives on Teaching World Englishes and English as a lingua franca. *TESOL Quarterly*, *40*(1), 157–181.

Kaur, J. (2010). Achieving mutual understanding in world Englishes. *World Englishes*, *29*(2), 192–208.

Kubota, R. (2018). Unpacking research and practice in world Englishes and second language acquisition. *World Englishes*, *37*, 93–105. doi: 10.1111/weng.12305.

Kuo, I. (2006). Addressing the issue of teaching English as a lingua franca. *ELT Journal*, *60*(3), 213–221. doi: 10.1093/elt/cc1001.

MacKenzie, I. (2014). *English as a lingua franca: Theorizing and teaching English*. Routledge.

Murray, N. (2012). English as a lingua franca and the development of pragmatic competence. *ELT Journal*, *66*(3), 318–326. doi: 10.1093/elt/ccso16.

Seidlhofer, B. (2004). Research perspectives on teaching English as a lingua franca. *Annual Review of Applied Linguistics*, *24*, 209–239. doi:10.1017.

Sowden, C. (2012). ELF on a mushroom: The overnight growth in English as a lingua franca. *ELT Journal*, *66*(1), 89–96. doi: 10.1093/elt/ccr024.

Sung, C.C.M. (2013). English as a lingua franca and English language teaching: A way forward. *ELT Journal*, *67*(3), 350–352. Doi: 10.1093/elt/cct015

Swan, M. (2017). ELF and the question of accuracy. *ELT Journal*, *71*(4), 511–515. doi: 10.1093/elt/ccx0311.

Further Reading

Crystal, D. (2012). *English as a global language (Second Edition)*. Canto

Classics.

Galloway, N. & Rose, H. (2015). *Introducing global Englishes*. Routledge.

Galloway, N. & Rose, H. (2019). *Global Englishes for language teaching*. Cambridge University Press.

Jenkins, J. (2015). *Global Englishes* (3rd Edition). Routledge English Language Introductions.

▌日本語文献案内

田中春美・田中幸子編『World Englishes：世界の英語への招待』昭和堂，2012 年.

本名信行・竹下裕子編著『世界の英語・私の英語：多文化共生社会をめざして』桐原書店，2018 年.

▌考えてみよう

以下の質問にできるだけ詳しく文章で答えてください.

1. Kachru は，世界で話されている英語の種類をどのように分類したのでしょうか？

2. ELF は，「インド英語」「アメリカ英語」「ナイジェリア英語」などの英語とどのように違うのか考えてください.

3. ジェンキンスとシードルホーファーの研究が，ELF の概念をどのように支えているか考えてください.

4. 教室での ELF 指導に対する批判について，どう思いますか.

5. 本文によると，21 世紀の学生に適した英語教育は，今後どのように変えていくべきでしょうか. あなたはこれに同意しますか？　詳細を書いてください.

マイケル・ジェームズ・デービス

Michael James DAVIES

英語のルーツとファンタジー文化

The Roots of English and Its Cultural Diversity: From Medieval Literature to Modern Fantasy

---

概要

　国際英語文化の土台である英語とはどのような言語でしょう. どこを発祥とし, どのように発達・発展してきたのでしょうか. もし読者の皆さんが, 英語をあくまでも語学として学んできた場合には, この種の問いについては考えてこなかったかもしれません. ただ, 人間の歩みは言葉の歴史と切り離すことはできません. この章では, 英語のルーツや発展に目を向けることで現代の英語文化の多様性を深く理解します.

　まず, 英語の歴史を紐解くことで, 現代英語を特色づける多様性の源流をたどります. 次に, 英語成立の初期に生まれた文学作品に触れ, それを現代のファン

図1　アーサー王物語──ファンタジーの源泉
[Sidney Lanier, ed,. *The Boy's King Arthur* (1920), 挿絵 N. C. Wyeth]

タジー文化と関連づけて説明します．古い時代の言語文化は決して過去の遺物などではなく，『指輪物語』や『ハリー・ポッター』シリーズなどの人気作品へと姿を変え，今日のファンタジー文化を彩る重要な素材の源になっています．本章は，英語の多文化性を歴史的にとらえることで言語文化を深く研究するための視点を提供します．

国際英語文化の中の英語ルーツとファンタジー文化研究

　何事も始まりを知ることは研究を行う上で欠かせません．研究対象を大きな歴史の中に位置づけることで，新たな知見や客観的視点が得られるからです．今や「グローバル」な言語となった英語も，もともときわめて「ローカル」な言葉でした．その事実を知れば，ではどうして英語は世界語になったのか，という問いが生まれるはずです．

　ルーツ探究の意義は，常に現代との関わりを探ることにあります．英語のルーツは，5世紀に大陸からブリテン島に移住した人々の言葉にさかのぼります．それはアングロ・サクソン人と呼ばれる一民族が話すローカルな言語にすぎませんでした．その後，キリスト教への改宗とともに文字を獲得し，複数の民族の侵入や異文化接触を経てさまざまに変化してきました．現在，英語は複数形で記される「英語変種」（"Englishes"）の時代へと突入し，「シングリッシュ」や「スパングリッシュ」など，従来の「ネイティブ」の手から離れ変幻自在な変化を遂げています．しかし通時的にみれば，この揺らぎと変容こそが今も昔も変わらない英語の本質といえるのです．

　英語の多彩な展開と同様に，中世ヨーロッパの言語文化も現代へ継承され，学術的領域だけでなく大衆文化にも浸透しています．例えば，『指輪物語』や『ナルニア国物語』，そして『ハリー・ポッター』シリーズなど，ファンタジー作品は科学技術が発達する以前の前近代的世界と深いつながりをもっています．ファンタジーというと現実とかけはなれた絵空事のように思うかもしれません．しかし，ハリー・ポッターが入学する「ホグワーツ魔法魔術学校」のような古めかしい独特の世界観は，実際は中世ヨーロッパをめぐる民族神話や歴史，そして文学伝統をもとにつくられています．おとぎ話や騎士道物語などは日本でも人気ですが，例えば，映画やゲームで繰り返し題材となる「アーサー王物語」も古代ブリテン島の先住民（ケルト系ブリトン人）の伝承にさかのぼります．神話や伝説は今も姿形を変えながら受け継がれ，多様な英語文化に彩りを与えています．

　このように，過去と現代の接点を紡ぐアプローチは，国際英語文化研究の醍醐味の1つです．

研究の楽しさ

　英語のルーツを学ぶことは，言葉の背後に潜む歴史文化を知る楽しみでもあります．そもそも，言葉は人の歩みを示す写し鏡のようなものです．多彩な語彙や言葉遣いは，人が紡ぎ出す文化そのものといっていいでしょう．例えば，英語を学習する中で，単語の多さに驚いた（辟易した）ことはありませんか．また，似通った意味をもつ語彙（＝類義語）にたびたび遭遇しませんか．意味が似ているからといってそれらを無作為に変換することはできません．使用場面や言葉同士の相性（collocation）など，文脈によってその響きは全然違ってきます．
　微妙な使い分けには歴史的背景が関係している場合があります．次の文章は，パーティーなどの催し物に「どのように迎えられたか」を表しています．

　・They gave us a hearty welcome.
　・They gave us a cordial reception.

　基本的な文意（「歓迎された」）は一緒ですが，浮かび上がる光景は異なります．前者はカジュアルに，後者はやや堅苦しく感じられます．この違いは "hearty welcome ／ cordial reception" からきています．"hearty welcome"（「温かく迎える」）は元来英語にあった語ですが，"cordial reception"（「真摯な応接を賜る」）はフランス語からの借用語です．
　実は，これらの単語のルーツが異なるニュアンスを生んでいます．11世紀の「ノルマン征服」は，フランスのノルマンディー公がイングランドを征服した出来事で，結果，島内の大部分はノルマン人の支配下に置かれました．彼らの言葉であったフランス語は宮廷や議会で使用される公的言語となり，土着の英語に取って代わりました．政治状況の転換によって両言語には文化的な格差が生まれました．英語の現状からすれば想像に難いかもしれませんが，かつて英語は被支配層の人々が話す社会的地位の低い言語だったのです．反対にフランス語は一種の権威を帯びた言語として，今も英語の語彙に多く残っています[1]．上記の2つの例文に戻ると，これらのニュアンスの違いには今から約1000年前の出来事が関係して

1　ノルマン征服以後，英語は公的権威をもたない一般庶民の言葉（＝「ヴァナキュラー言語」）となっていた．ヴァナキュラーについては3章を参照のこと．また，ここで紹介した例文については，TED-Ed (November 2012) "How did English evolve?" (by Kate Gardoqui) [https://ed.ted.com/lessons/how-did-english-evolve-kate-gardoqui] を視聴のこと．また，Simeon Potter は著書の中で，"We feel more at ease after getting a *hearty welcome* than after being granted a *cordial reception*" (37-8) と書いている．

いることがわかるでしょう.

この章のトピック

　本章は, 英語のルーツ研究と現代のファンタジー文化研究の2つから構成されます. 両研究における共通項は, やはり歴史的知見の大切さです. ブリテン島は, ときに「侵略の歴史」といわれるほど, 度重なる異民族の侵攻を受けました. 英語は他言語との接触・摩擦の中で発展してきたのです. 現代英語を構成する語彙の語源 ("etymology" =語のルーツ) の割合をみてみましょう. 何と, 英語が属するゲルマン語系は, 約60万語といわれる語彙全体の約4分の1でしかありません. 代わりに, ラテン語やフランス語などの「外国語」が半分以上を占めています (例えば, language や culture などの日常的語彙はそもそも英語ではありません). これは英語が他国の言語を取り入れ, 異文化との交流を通して成立したことを如実に示しています. そしてその営みは今も世界各地で展開し, 変容の歩みを続けているのです.

　英語の伝来とともに, 中世イギリスではブリテン島に移住した民族の物語が語り継がれました. 文字の芸術である「文学」は英語の発展には欠かせない「文化物」です. 特に中世の文学・文化は, 現代のファンタジー世界を彩る題材を提供しています. 例えば, 英語で書かれた最古の物語詩 (叙事詩) に『ベーオウルフ』(成立は8～11世紀と諸説分かれる) という作品がありますが, これはベーオウルフという勇者によるモンスター退治の逸話です. 若き戦士ベーオウルフは, 隣国を悩ます怪物グレンデルとその母親女怪を討ち, 50年後老王となってもなお, 故国を襲うドラゴンと戦い名誉の死を遂げます. ファンタジー色の強い英雄譚は英語文学の紛れもないルーツの1つなのです. また, 英雄とモンスターが戦いを繰り広げる舞台も特筆されます. 英語文学の始まりと聞けば当然, 母国イングランドあるいはブリテン島を思い浮かべるでしょう. 実は本作の舞台は海を隔てた北欧の一帯です. 当時の聴衆は大陸で勲を立てる祖先の武勇に耳を傾け, 胸を躍らせたことでしょう. 大陸からブリテン島へ移住した英語話者はその後世界各地へ進出し, 彼らの言葉は人種や国籍を超え世界の共通語へと変容しました. 英語文学の原風景には, 「ローカル」から「グローバル」な展開を占う豊かな素地をすでに確認することができます.

研究の素材

　英語を基盤として展開する文学・文化はすべて研究の素材となります．特に，英語のルーツであるイングランド（あるいはイギリス）を端緒とし，今日に至るまで影響を与えている文芸や文化事象に注目してみてください．一例として，「アーサー王物語」を挙げてみましょう．現在，アーサー王物語に由来する題材（円卓，聖杯，魔法使いマーリンなど）は日本の大衆文化に浸透し，西洋ファンタジーの１つのイメージを形成しています．ただ，今ではファンタジー色の強いアーサー王物語もブリテン島の先住民の間で語り継がれていた１つの歴史物語でした．アーサーは当初，王ではなく，大陸から侵攻した異民族と戦った一介の戦士にすぎませんでした（ケルト系のアーサーはむしろ「英語文化」の侵入に抗った人物なのです）．この人物にまつわる断片的な逸話は時代を経て，史実とフィクションの織り成す膨大な物語群へと発展していきました．ブリテン島の支配をめぐる歴史的・民族的遺産が今日のファンタジー文化へと生まれ変わり，マンガやアニメ，ゲームなど多くの文芸創作のインスピレーションとなっています．中世の言語文化は時代や地域に応じてさまざまに受容され，改変され，新たな創作の活力となっているのです．英語に関する素材はこうした文化伝承・文化変容の視点から見ることが可能です[2]．

研究がめざすこと

　英語のルーツ研究やファンタジー文化研究では，言葉への感性を磨き，多様な英語文化を深く理解することをめざします．物事の多様性が叫ばれる今日，世界中で用いられている英語はその象徴的な１つでしょう．しかし，英語の多様化は決して今に始まったことではありません．これまでみてきたように，英語やファンタジーの歴史的発展には元来，多数の地域の民族・文化が関わってきました．過去から現代へ，あるいは現代から過去へ——特定の地域や時間軸にとらわれることなく，ダイナミックに想像力を働かせて言葉と文化を研究すれば，今まで見えてなかった世界が見えるはずです．

2　英語や英語文学の通時的な研究には，『オックスフォード英語辞典』（*The Oxford English Dictionary*, 通称 *OED*）が有益である．本辞書では英語の語すべての「来歴」を調べることができる．これに関しては 9 章を参照のこと．

The Roots of English and Its Cultural Diversity: From Medieval Literature to Modern Fantasy

TABLE OF CONTENTS

1. Introduction

English is now a global language. It is widely used around the world. Do you know that it was originally a *local* language spoken only in a particular area? Where does English come from and how did it develop? For those who have learned English merely as a tool for conversation, these kinds of question might not have come to mind. The language we use has changed over time, just as humans have throughout history. In this section, we will explore the origins of English and its cultural diversity. We will then look at literary works in the Middle Ages and study their significance in relation to modern fantasy fiction. Overall, we will gain a deeper understanding of the English language and culture from a historical point of view.

2. The Origins of "English" and its Cultural Diversity

Roots of English

Where did English come from? Some may say America, while others *Igirisu* in Japanese. If these are the two choices, the latter is closer to the right answer. Yet, you need to be careful using the term, as *Igirisu* is usually a collective term for the four countries that make up the United Kingdom: England, Wales, Scotland, and Northern Ireland. In this case, Japanese *Igirisu* has little to do with the origin of English, nor does the UK.

The origin of the word "English" goes back to "England" not *Igirisu* (which is from Portuguese *Inglez* referring to "England"). The name "England" comes from the name of an ethnic group, and originally referred to "the land of the Angles" (derived from "Engla-land"). The Angles were the ancestors of English speakers, one of the Germanic tribes who lived in the Anglia

Peninsula (*Angeln* in Schleswig-Holstein, Germany) located in the southern part of the Jutland Peninsula (where Denmark is now). As part of the so-called Germanic migrations, the Angles arrived in Britain in the mid-5th century with other tribes called Saxons and Jutes (afterward, these tribes together came to be called "Anglo-Saxons"). Thus, traced back to its ultimate roots, the English homeland was neither the U.K. nor "England," but the continent across from Britain. Only a small number of local people spoke the language during the time of these migrations.

The original English, introduced to the island in the 5th century, is called "Old English." This Anglo-Saxon native language laid the foundation for today's English (called "Present-Day English"). In general, English passed through the following stages of development:

Old English	450 ～ 1100
Middle English	1100 ～ 1500
Modern English	1500 ～ 1900
Present-Day English	1900 ～ present

Looking at this table, it appears from the sequence of names that English developed in a straight line without any particular break. However, this continuity is only a reflection of people's thinking, a historical division for convenience set by later people. People in the "Old English" and "Middle English" periods did not name the English they used that way. The historical continuity suggests that the language plays a role in being "English." English was not only a means of personal communication but also an idea deeply involved in the creation of national unity and identity. In other words, the apparent historical continuity is nothing but a desire to claim an identity, and unfortunately, this claim is sometimes not true to reality.

Cultural Diversity

It should be noted that English has never been a single language. For nearly 1500 years, the language has shaped a linguistic identity through contact with various countries, ethnic groups, and languages. Perhaps the claim of continuity was another side of an anxiety over English speaker's native tongue. Although its present status as a global language might make it hard to imagine, English has long carried a sense of linguistic inferiority compared with Western classical languages. For example, Latin was the language of the Roman Catholic Church and learning. It was imported mainly through the spread of Christianity at the end of the 6th century and continued to be the English ecclesiastical language for many centuries. Even prior to Christianization, Anglo-Saxons had language contact with the native inhabitants of the land— the Celts. Celtic Britons left very few words in English, mostly place names: *London*, *Thames*, and *Avon*. Above all, the name "Britain" itself originates from the Latin name for the land of the Britons, or indigenous Celtic people!

In the 8th century, the Vikings, Scandinavian adventurers, started to harass the English and settled in part of the island. Their language, Old Norse, also influenced English in many ways. From the beginning, English has constantly been not only in touch with outsiders, but also in danger of the loss of identity due to the repeated intrusions of different peoples. The path from "local" to "global" was a bumpy road and is sometimes referred to as a history of invasion. Here, history has left a lasting imprint on the vocabulary. Let us look at words that have flowed into English through contact with other ethnic groups. Words taken from abroad are called "borrowings."

The pie chart shows the proportions of "etymology" (the roots of words) from other languages in the vocabulary that makes up English. It is surprising that the lexicon of "Germanic Languages," to which English belongs, accounts for only 26% of the total (about 600,000 words). "Latin" and "French" account for more than half, and this means that many components of Present-Day English are made up of foreign (non-Germanic) words. French is one of the languages that descended from Latin, the official language of the Roman Empire. Languages such as French, Italian, Spanish, Portuguese, and Romanian are grouped as "romance languages" because they are all descended from that of the "Romans."

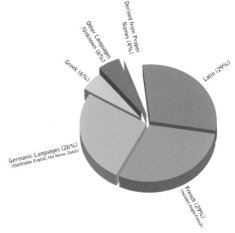

Figure 1　Etymology of modern English words [Wikimedia Commons]

Let us pick French out of these and consider why its words occupy almost one-third of the whole vocabulary. One major factor is an event called the "Norman Conquest" in 1066. This was the conquest of England by William, the Duke of Normandy in north-western France, who claimed succession to the English throne. As a result, most of the island came under Norman control, and their language, French, became officially used in administration, courts, and the government, as well as among the upper class. This change in political and social structure led to many French words coming into English, creating semantic differences in pairs such as "pig/pork," "cow/beef," and "sheep/mutton." In each pair, the former is an English word used among peasants (the colonized) to refer to the animal in the field, while the latter is the French word for the animal, used among the nobility (the colonizers) to refer to its meat. The different usage of words still remains today. While English went "underground" in the wake of the Norman dominion, it gradually regained power. It continues to absorb words from various languages, much like a sponge, and grows flexibly. In the long run, contact with others like the Normans might have been "a blessing in disguise" that allowed the English language to expand its scope and taste.[3]

The way English turned global is a trajectory of change and breakthrough from local to global, from monolingual to multilingual. Regarding the overseas spread of English, we need to consider several events in modern history, such as the discovery of new continents, colonialism, British industrialization, the rise of America as the economic power in the 20th century, and advances in science and technology more recently. Nevertheless, we cannot forget the potential soil for diversity that was formed in the early days of English through cultural interactions with other people. Thus, the historical perspective of the shape of English deepens the understanding of the ethnic and cultural imprints of the English-speaking world.

3. Medieval Literature and the World of Fantasy
Medieval Literature and Fantasy

The basis of English was developed in the early ages of history, and what is often hailed as cultural diversity is not a recent phenomenon. In order to

---

3   English is often described as having "cosmopolitan vocabularies." For the details, see Baugh and Cable, pp. 9-10.

enrich our understanding of English, this section examines the nature of literary works produced in the period. There is no doubt that linguistic development is hardly separable from literary creations. Here, it is important to note that, while "literature" is sometimes considered to be based on creative imagination, it is also a "cultural artifact." It is a cultural creation woven mainly by words. In earlier stages of English history, many stories were first told by word of mouth, and only written down in manuscripts ("books" made of animal skin) after the introduction of "letters" through Christianity. Thus, literature is an art of words.

The literary works produced in the Old and Middle English periods are grouped as "medieval" English literature. "Medieval" is an interesting word. It is an adjective related to the term "Middle Ages." The Middle Ages is one of the historical divisions used in Western countries, a period ranging roughly from the 5th to the 15th century ("usually taken as extending from the fall of the Roman Empire in the West [c500] to the fall of Constantinople [1453] or the beginning of the Renaissance [14th century]").[4] These years are situated in the "middle," a period between "ancient" and "modern." When you hear something "medieval" (「中世の」), you may get the impression of its being slightly old-fashioned and inaccessible. On the other hand, it may also evoke an otherworld of mystery and fantasy (especially when you hear the phrase 「中世風・中世ヨーロッパ風」), where fairies, dragons, or wizards turn up. The Middle Ages are not only a certain historical period, but also carry a sense of wonder and charm.[5]

Medieval English literature has a number of such fascinating stories. In fact, one of the oldest surviving poems in English is the story of a hero who kills a monster and dragon! This is a poem of 3,182 lines of verse, titled *Beowulf*, composed around the 8th to 11th centuries (theories vary). The poem belongs to the so-called "epic" genre, a narrative defined by heroic or legendary adventures.[6] *Beowulf* begins with the story of a young brave warrior Be-

---

4　*The Oxford English Dictionary*, s.v. "middle age."

5　Regarding the image of the Middle Ages and its reception in Japan, see 岡本 .

6　Interestingly, the poem is set in Scandinavia (apparently in the 6th century), not in England (or Britain). It opens with a brief genealogy of the Danish royal dynasty. Seamus Heaney's modern English translation goes as follows: "So. The Spear-Danes in days gone by / and the kings who ruled them had courage and greatness. / We have heard of those princes' heroic campaigns" (ll.1-3).

owulf, who came to save the king of the Danes from the monster Grendel. After the defeat of Grendel, Beowulf also killed Grendel's mother, as she sought to revenge for her son. In the second half of the epic, after the hero returns to his homeland and becomes an old king, he fights and slays a fire dragon attacking his country, and finally dies in honor.

Legends and adventures of the heroes as well as monsters are popular themes in the modern genre called "fantasy." In fact, medieval images and materials are also often used in novels, films, and video games. The following chart shows the best-selling fantasy book series of all times[7]:

the Best-Selling Fantasy Books and Series of All Time		
1	*Harry Potter* Series (1997–2007) by J.K. Rowling	450 million
2	*The Lord of the Rings* (1954–55) by J. R. R. Tolkien	150 million
3	*The Hobbit* (1937) by J. R. R. Tolkien	142 million
4	*Le Petit Prince* (1943) by Antoine de Saint-Exupéry	140 million
5	*The Chronicles of Narnia* (1950) by C. S. Lewis	120 million

Among them, J. R. R. Tolkien's *The Hobbit*, released as a film trilogy in recent years, and its sequel *The Lord of the Rings*; C.S. Lewis's *The Chronicles of Narnia*; and, more recently, J.K. Rowling's *Harry Potter* series recorded explosive sales worldwide and became a kind of social phenomenon. As shown in the success of the *Harry Potter* series, the fantasy genre is already familiar to a wide range of generations from children to adults.

One of the characteristics of the fantasy genre is that its primary setting tends to be somewhat different, temporally distant from the present. While science fiction (SF) is oriented towards the future, fantasy prefers to look back into the past. Here, medieval elements are related to the formation of the fantasy genre. J.R.R. Tolkien (1892–1973) is generally regarded as the forerunner of the contemporary fantasy boom and is a representative "fantasy writer." However, his occupation was professor at Oxford University, with the titles "Rawlinson and Bosworth Professor of Anglo-Saxon" (1925–45) and "Merton Professor of English Language and Literature" (1945–59). As shown by the word "Anglo-Saxon," he is an academic who specialized in medieval language and literature. Tolkien also worked with C.S. Lewis (1898–1963), a

---

7   The chart is based on Nicola Alter's observation. See the details: https://thoughtsonfantasy.com/2016/06/15/what-are-the-best-selling-fantasy-books-and-series-of-all-time/

scholar who loved classical and medieval stories, and who wrote the seven-part fantasy masterpiece, *The Chronicles of Narnia*. Considering their popular influence, it is possible to say that their academic background as "medieval-ists" created a template for the modern fantasy world. As a fan of Lewis's work, Rowling commented, "I found myself thinking about the wardrobe route to Narnia when Harry is told he has to hurl himself at a barrier in Kings Cross Station—it dissolves and he's on platform Nine and Three-Quarters, and there's the train for Hogwarts."[8] The different (parallel) world of Hogwarts School of Witchcraft and Wizardry is full of mythical creatures and medieval elements, such as magic, castle and dungeon, heraldry, and forbidden forests.

The Story of King Arthur

Finally, this paper ends by introducing one of the medieval stories that these fantasy writers all favored, the story of King Arthur. The legend of King Arthur is well-known today and you might have heard of some of the related items and terms, such as "Excalibur," "the knights of the Round Table," and "the Holy Grail." There are also various adaptations, such as Walt Disney's animated version *The Sword in the Stone* (1963) and *First Knight* (1995), a film starring Sean Connery (Arthur) and Richard Gere (Lancelot). Its popularity goes beyond time and space, and Japan is no exception.

Who was Arthur? Originally, he was not a king. The story of Arthur was told orally and enjoyed by the ancient Celtic people (native inhabitants of Britain). His name was first recorded in the chronicle of a battle for the rule of Britain. Arthur was a military leader who won many victories against the Anglo-Saxon invaders, using superpowers to defeat hundreds of enemies at one charge. Thus, Arthur was originally on the side resisting the intrusion of the English language and culture. As we have seen, the pendulum of history swung towards Anglo-Saxon rule, and the Britons were driven to the margins of the island in such areas as Scotland, Wales, and Cornwall.

After the 12th century, people started to enlarge the story and made him a king of Britain (and England afterwards, ironically), who even embarked on

---

8   Jennie Renton. "The story behind the Potter legend: JK Rowling talks about how she created the Harry Potter books and the magic of Harry Potter's world". *Sydney Morning Herald*. Retrieved 28 Feb, 2021.

military campaigns to the continent and finally took the throne of the Roman emperor. The secret of his birth was also added, in which the power of Merlin the magician helped his father (Uther Pendragon) to marry another man's wife to bear him. Arthur was a son who was born to a marriage by deception (Merlin's magic) and abduction! He was taken away by Merlin so young that he grew up without knowing his lineage (does this remind you of Harry Potter?). King Arthur's reputation immediately spread across Western Europe, being received and rewritten in various ways. Many related stories blossomed combining both historical facts and fiction. Attention has been increasingly paid to the deeds of individual knights: Gawain, Lancelot, Tristan, Percival, and so forth. They not only support the king but also the cultural longevity of the tale itself.

Figure 2　The Sword in the Stone[ウォルト・ディズニー・プロダクション／販売元ブエナ・ビスタ・ホーム・エンターテイメント, 2006]

In this way, one of the attractions of Arthurian legend is its interesting reception and the flowering of diverse versions. Sometimes people are eager to know whether Arthur really existed or not, yet vague historicity provides a more fruitful soil for new creations than the solid fact. It is important to note that most of the Arthurian story can be considered fantasy, but rooted in history. There was no such figure as Arthur who, despite his legendary status, has been hugely popular from the Middle Ages through the 21st century. After the 18th and 19th centuries, when medieval society was idealized in response to growing industrialization, interest in vernacular cultures, such as traditional folklore and local ballads, increased. The Celtic legacy of the Arthurian tale captured attention, serving as an inspiration for literary and artistic movements.[9] A series of cultural movements and attempts to rework medieval ingredients is termed "medievalism." The Arthurian legend has been one of the vital sources of medievalism and continues to appeal to popular imagination.

9　For example, just prior to winning the Nobel prize in Literature 2017, Japan-born British novelist Kazuo Ishiguro wrote *The Buried Giant* in 2016, which features the Arthurian world. He actually took its inspiration from one of the medieval Arthurian masterpieces *Sir Gawain and the Green Knight*.

4. Conclusion

This chapter explored the roots of English and its cultural diversity in connection with the present. It also discussed an aspect of medieval literature and its popular reception as fantasy. Facing and reading the past is a kind of dialogue (or communication) with the ancestors who walked before us. This is important for understanding the diverse culture that lies deep in today's English-speaking world. When studying an original text, it is necessary to obtain historical knowledge of English itself. If you wish to develop the power of international communication, it is vital to cultivate your sensitivity to the history of language and culture.

▌References

岡本広毅「ファンタジーの世界と RPG：新中世主義の観点から」『立命館言語文化研究』31 巻 1 号，175-187，2019.

Baugh, Albert C. and Thomas Cable. *A History of the English Language*. 6th ed. London: Routledge, 2013.

Heaney, Seamus. *Beowulf: A New Verse Translation*. Norton & Company, 2001.

The Oxford English Dictionary. 2nd ed. 1989. *OED Online*. www.oed.com

Potter, Simeon. *Our Language*. Rev. ed. Penguin. 1990.

▌Further Reading

Horobin, Simon. *How English Became English: A Short History of a Global Language*. Oxford University Press, 2016.

Ishiguro, Kazuo. *The Buried Giant*. Faber & Faber, 2015.

Svartvik, Jan, et al. *English: One Tongue, Many Voices*. 2nd ed., Palgrave Macmillan, 2006.

Tolkien, J. R. R., trans. *Sir Gawain and the Green Knight, Pearl, and Sir Orfeo*, edited by Christopher Tolkien, HarperCollins, 1995.

▌日本語文献案内

安藤聡『ファンタジーと英国文化：児童文学王国の名作をたどる』彩流社，2019 年.

岡本広毅・小宮真樹子編『いかにしてアーサー王は日本で受容されサブカルチャー界に君臨したか：変容する中世騎士道物語』みずき書林，2019 年.

サイモン・ウィンチェスター／鈴木主税訳『博士と狂人：世界最高の辞書 OED の誕生秘話』早川書房，2006 年.

ステファニー・L. バーチェフスキー／野崎嘉信・山本洋訳『大英帝国の伝説：
　アーサー王とロビン・フッド』法政大学出版局，2005 年.
堀田隆一『はじめての英語史：英語の「なぜ？」に答える』研究社，2016 年.

▌考えてみよう

1.　18 世紀の文人サミュエル・ジョンソンは最初の本格的な英語辞書（1755）
　　を作成しました．この辞書で "English"（形容詞）は以下のように定義され
　　ています．この語義はあなたの考える英語の意味と同じですか．違いますか.
　　違う場合はなぜ違うのか考えてみましょう.

> Énglish. adj. [enʒles, Saxon.] Belonging to England; thence English
> is the language of England.

2.　身近なポピュラー・カルチャーにある "medievalism"（「中世主義」）を取
　　り上げ，中世の素材がどのように用いられているか考えてみましょう.

....

岡本　広毅
Hiroki OKAMOTO

ヴァナキュラー文学，歌と物語

A Short Introduction to Vernacular Literature:
What is It and How is It Interesting?

概要

　この章では，文学と文化を研究することについて説明します．文学は文化の一部なのですが，図書館の分類でいう〈文学〉の研究が進んだ一方，文学研究はその器である〈文化〉を見ることを忘れがちでした．しかし20世紀の後半からは，文学を「言葉による人間の営み」としてとらえ直そうという動きが活発です．文学を生活に密着したものと考えるときには，歌や物語など，声と言葉による創作が特に大事になります．そこでここでは，声を媒介に表現され伝承された声の文学とそのリメイク版を合わせて，「ヴァナキュラー文学」というカテゴリーで扱います．Vernacularは，日常に根ざしたものにつける形容詞で，詳しくは英文の説明を読んでください．「ヴァナキュラー文学」には，歌詞や物語，伝説，辻説教や芸人の口上など多様なものが含まれ，リメイク版も研究対象になります．

図1　Illustration from the 1855 edition of La Fontaine's *Fables* ［Public Domain］

国際英語文化の中のヴァナキュラー文学研究

外国語を学ぶと，言葉の知識と同時に人々の習慣や思考，価値観も知ることができます．また逆に，人々についてある程度の知識と理解がなければ，外国語を快適に使うことはできません．コミュニケーションには〈言語〉と〈人々のすること〉の知識が両輪として必要です．「言語を使って人々のすること」の洗練されたものが〈文学〉であり，「人々のすること」の総体が〈文化〉です．

英語が世界の共通言語となった現在，英語で人々がしてきたこと，とりわけ歌ったり話したり演じたりという声での言語活動で仕上げられた作品（＝ヴァナキュラー文学）の，生い立ちや変容を知ると，文化としての英語の性格がよくわかります．時代とともに何が新しくなり，何が変わらず生き続けたのか．日本で世代を超えて愛され続ける英語の歌があるとして，その理由はなぜか．こうしたことを考えるのは，英語を使用する人々と私たちがコミュニケーションするための大切な努力であり，私たちが英語でよりよく意志疎通するためにも重要なことです．

研究の楽しさ

ヴァナキュラー文学研究の面白さに，作品の背後にある大きな世界と多様な人々を実感できる点があります．

少し話が飛ぶようですが，読者は日本文化をどれほど〈独自〉であると考えますか．アメリカは移民国だから多文化だけれど日本文化は独自だ，という議論を時々耳にします．しかし，本当にそうでしょうか．日本と中国は尖閣諸島の領有権をめぐってなかなか折り合えません．これに象徴されるように，現代では国の境界は政治的に取り決められます．「日本」という国は，極端な言い方をすれば，1つの取り決めでしかありません．一方で，そこに住む人々は国籍はどうあれ実態として存在し，各集団には何かしら特徴的な文化があります．その上，文化は人の移動とともに交流を繰り返すので，完全な独自性を保つことは滅多にありません．

日本の文化も，古くから大陸文化を積極的に取り入れつつ形成されたもので，明治以降は欧米文化を歓迎してきましたから，領土外から受けた影響がとても大きいのです．それでも便宜的に「日本文化」と呼べるものはあります．ただそれを〈外〉の文化と完全に切り分けて観察するのは，文化研究にはなじまない姿勢です．日常的な言語のアートは人とともに移動し，今ではインターネット上で瞬

時に伝達され新たな文化を次々に生み出しています．世界共通語になった英語を利用して横断的に文化を観察すると，人間の共通性と独自性の両方がよく見えます．

　話をヴァナキュラー文学に戻しましょう．声を使って表現される言語アートは作者が意識されにくく，特に古い作品には版権がないので自由につくり直されて，異なるバージョンが生まれます．リメイク版とか "パクリ" とか呼ばれるこうしたバリエーションを比べると，文化の広がりと変容を知ることができます．その動きに，私は「人間とは何か」を洞察できる気がして楽しいのですが，読者もきっと価値ある面白いことを発見するでしょう．

この章のトピック

　研究の一例として，本章では「ウサギと亀」のバリエーションを紹介，分析します．歌もありますね．童謡は，1901（明治 34）年に出版された『幼年唱歌二編上巻』に載りました．

　さて「ウサギと亀」の話では，瞬時に自己発揮する能力者よりも地道な努力者が勝利するという道徳的な教えが明らかです．これは明治時代から小学校で国語の教科書を通して教育され，国民も好んで受入れたモラルでした．ところが世界には，異なる理解に基づくバリエーションがあります．

　「ウサギと亀」の寓話[1]は，紀元前 600 年から 500 年頃ギリシャでイソップが語り伝えたとされています．伝承寓話ですが紀元前からすでに書き記され，語り直されたり書き直されたりして現代に伝わっています．イソップは，自らの怠惰を戒めて自己研鑽することの大事さを伝えたかったようです．

　イソップの「ウサギと亀」の英訳で広く流布している 19 世紀のバージョンは，私たちが知っているものと大筋は変わりありません．しかし私たちになじみのない追加もあります．亀はウサギに侮辱されたので，自らの名誉をかけて挑戦したのだという点と，審判として別の動物が選ばれている点です．名誉が大事である決闘は立会人のもとに行われるという西欧の習慣が，付け加えられています．そして〈勝者になること〉がテーマとして前に押し出されています．

　この話はアメリカの黒人たちにも言い伝えられ，大きく変化しました．ジュリアス・レスター再話による現代版（1999）では，題名は「ウサギ君がとうとう負けるお話」です．この話では色々なことがひっくり返っています．どんなに勤勉に働いても日の目を見ない亀のような立場の人々は，知恵と団結によって強者

1　たとえ話．登場人物を動物にして，人間社会を風刺したものが多い．

を出し抜くというのが，黒人バージョンのモラルとしてあります．

レスターが再話したバージョンには，もとになった物語が2種類あります．1つは，アフリカから連れてこられた人々がアメリカ南部で奴隷にされていたときから語られていた伝承話です．もう1つは，アフリカ民話「亀とハヤブサ」です．何世代もアメリカにいてアフリカの言語も生活の記憶も失っているのに，物語や歌の中には民族の文化が生き続けていました．ヴァナキュラー文学の研究は，歴史の動きと人々の生き様とを教えてくれるのです．

研究の素材

私自身の研究素材は，歌や物語です．他の研究素材も「言葉のアート」であれば無限にあるでしょう．ヴァナキュラー文学研究では，どのような作品とバリエーションを，何を基準に類似のカテゴリーに切り取るかが重要です．新しい研究分野なので，固定した研究素材のイメージがまだありません．研究対象は自分のアンテナで探し当て，大事な要素を複合的に判断してカテゴリー化します．楽しいけれども難しい作業です．従来の文学研究は文字作品を「文学」としてカテゴライズし，図書館や資料館にある文献と手紙や日記などを研究素材としてきました．しかしヴァナキュラー文学研究では，声で発せられて消えてしまう歌や伝承物語，巧みな呼び込みの宣伝文句，替え歌なども研究素材とみなします．大量に存在する研究素材をどう集め，グループ分けし，解釈して意味づけるかというプロセスのすべてが，研究する者の個性や分析力にかかっています．

研究がめざすこと

では，資料分析で大事なことは何でしょうか．学術研究の出発点は，当たり前とされていることに疑いをもつところにあります．例えば「良いは悪い，悪いは良い」という一見矛盾した世界が，文学の中には存在します．矛盾を含む世界こそが，私たちの現実なのだと文学は教えてくれます．

なぜ社会の表層で使われる言葉は，現実をより正確に伝えようとする複雑な表現を嫌い，疑問を挟まない表現になるのか．それは，常識や共通の感性が社会の秩序を守る一方で，人々の疑問は摩擦や変革の種になるからです．「良いは悪い，悪いは良い」がまかり通ったら，世の中は混乱してしまいますね．「この戦争は正しい」と主張する人は，戦争に疑問をもたせる話はしないはずです．しかし文学は，世界の隠れた秘密事をささやきます．したがって，文学の深さを楽しむに

は，まず読者が既成の概念を脱ぐ必要があります．多様な世界の〈可能性を受入れる〉ところから，研究が始まります．

　書き言葉の文学を大衆が楽しむようになったのは，長い人類の歴史からすればごく最近のことです．近代教育を採用した国々で，労働者階級の人々が日常的に文字を読み書きするようになるのは 19 世紀です．人類史上人口の大半が読み書きできるようになるまでの長い間，また読み書きが普及してからも，人々は集って物語りをしたり聞いたり歌ったりして，声と耳とで言葉のアートを楽しんでいました．

　声の文学は，日常に根ざした楽しみを生命としています．それは私たちの苦痛を和らげ，幸せな気持ちにし，よりよく生きる方法を教えてくれる〈身体的な言葉のエッセンス〉なのです．読者の皆さん，ヴァナキュラー文学研究の世界へようこそ．

A Short Introduction to Vernacular Literature: What is It and How is It Interesting?

TABLE OF CONTENTS

1.　Introduction

Literature is one of the major disciplines of humanities. It is a field of study about words and languages, and you may think that literature can be shared only among those who can write and read books. This is true of "authored" works (created first in writing), but there is another kind of literature, called "vernacular literature." Vernacular literature includes artistic works of language expressed orally: songs, tales, jokes, satire, epic, folk ritual chants, and more. The study of vernacular literature handles these genres, along with literary adaptations made from them. Vernacular literature also includes modern works made for entertainment, such as the Disney films of *Cinderella* (1950 by Walt Disney Productions, 1997 by Walt Disney Television, and 2015 by Walt Disney Pictures).

2. Basic Concepts of Vernacular Literature
What do we mean by "vernacular"?

We can think about this in two ways:

a. *Spoken vs. written language.* "Vernacular language" is the everyday spoken language you use, but is not limited to local dialect. The Japanese language that you speak in school or at home is vernacular, while the classical Japanese in the *Tale of Genji* is not. The formal language of law is not vernacular, either.

b. *Community vs. standard language.* Dialect, or the language used particularly among a certain group of people, is more vernacular than standard/official language.

And then, what is "literature"? This is a big question. Scholars have different answers, but generally "literature" in this context indicates the "art of language." It is expressed in both oral and written forms,[2] and is enjoyed in both private communities and more formal settings.[3]

The Divine Comedy by Dante Alighieri (1265-1321) and *The Canterbury Tales* by Geoffrey Chaucer (1342/43-1400) are examples of one type of vernacular literature. They were written in Italian and English, respectively, when literature was supposed to be written in Latin. At that time, Italian and English were vernacular languages[4]. Another type of vernacular literature isn't written at all but is spoken. Songs and stories are good examples. Works of this type were created mostly by uneducated people for the purposes of entertaining themselves or teaching useful things to each other. This vernacular verbal art appears and disappears instantly unless people remember and transmit it orally or record it in writing.

Most vernacular language art had been preserved orally for hundreds of years. In modern times, a great number of valuable works are transcribed, while some are audio-visually recorded. Scholars study these texts or record-

---

2   Literature expressed orally includes song lyrics, tales/stories, folk religious chants. These belong to vernacular literature. Literature expressed originally in writing includes novels and poetry.

3   Here, "private community" refers to a functional group, such as an online community, workplace community, or student community. Examples of formal settings are school, library, government television network, and so on.

4   Vernacular language here means the spoken language (日常語) while Latin was the official common language for writing (筆記語) in Europe.

ings and their adaptations, as well.

In sum, there are broadly four types of vernacular literature we can study:

(1) *works written in vernacular language*, such as *The Divine Comedy* and *The Canterbury Tales*

(2) *works originally spoken but written later*, such as folktales and epics

(3) *works adapted from vernacular literature*

(4) *works created using the vernacular of our time*

How is vernacular literature different from authored written literature?

This is a difficult question to answer. Let me ask you to do a small task. List ten songs you like and write down some of the lyrics on a sheet of paper. Tell someone why you like them, what's good about the words, and how important they are to you. Song lyrics are vernacular literature; you enjoy them repeatedly, transmit them when you speak to your friends about the songs, and you may even change the words when you sing. Vernacular literature lives with you and allows you to reshape it for yourself.

Authored written literature, on the other hand, claims the genius of the author. Here is another task. List ten novels or poems you like very much, and then write down a passage from each. You may be able to do this easily if you are a literature lover, but for most of you, 10 favorite lyrics are easier to list than ten literature passages. Written literature was treasured only by certain people such as aristocrats and scholars until the 20th century, when schooling became normal for most people. In the 21st century, it is distanced again from our daily life while people have many types of entertainment and self-education systems besides reading books of literature.

There is no clear border, however, between vernacular literature and authored written literature. Both present the art of language and give us pleasure in life. Both also provide important information to enrich our thoughts and emotions. Neither of them is more valuable than the other. Besides, written literature cannot be created without vernacular elements, and vernacular literature cannot be refined to the level of art without the knowledge of written literature.

What is interesting about vernacular literature?

Let's go back to the question I asked above; why do you like the ten songs you listed? I guessed the answer was "you enjoy them repeatedly, transmit them when you speak to your friends about the songs, and you may even change the words when you sing to fit better to your own feeling." These three things are major elements that make vernacular literature interesting: enjoyable, transmittable, and adaptable.

Out of the three elements, the last two work together and keep vernacular literature alive for many years. Take, for example, an Aesop's fable, "The Tortoise and the Hare." Aesop was a slave who lived in Greece around the late 600s and early 500s BCE (Nakatsukasa 365); not much is known about him, though. Aesop never wrote down his fables himself, but they were passed from mouth to mouth. Scholars believe that "The Tortoise and the Hare" wasn't transcribed until sometime during the 1st or 2nd century (Nakatsukasa 360). This means that the story was transmitted orally among anonymous people for 600 or 700 years after Aesop, and years before Aesop's birth, as Aesop must have learned the story from others.

"The Tortoise and the Hare" came to be well-known in the late 19th century Japan when it was cited in the government-approved elementary Japanese reading textbooks, and in the lyrics of the school-taught song "Usagi to Kame." Since then, "The Tortoise and the Hare" has been well-loved in Japan. It is retold in children's books as well as used in various types of parodies. Likewise, the story has evolved or been adapted in other cultures. It is very interesting to look into the differences and commonalities of variations and to think about their meanings.

3. The Network of Vernacular Literature
Aesop's fables and a Japanese textbook version

First, let's read "The Tortoise and the Hare" by Japanese translation from *Augustanus Monacensis 564* (a medieval manuscript). The story is simple, and the moral[5] (*kyōkun*) of the story is clear.

> 亀と兎が足の速さのことで言い争い，勝負の日時と場所を決めて別れた．さて，ウサギは生まれつき足が速いので，真剣に走らず，道から外れて眠り込んだが，亀は自分の遅いのを知っているので，たゆまず走り続け，ウサギ

---

5 A "moral" of a story is a practical lesson/teaching that you learn from the story. It is kyōkun 教訓 in Japanese.

が横になっているところも通り過ぎて，勝利のゴールに到達した.
素質も磨かなければ努力に負けることが多い，ということをこの話は解き
明かしている.（Perry Tale # 226, Nakatukasa 174）[6]

Japanese people welcomed Aesop's Fables in the Meiji era as textbook materials suited to the newly Westernized school system. The Japanese elementary school version of "The Tortoise and the Hare" was cited in *Shōgakudokuhon
Shotōka, Kan-yon*『小学読本 初等科 巻四』in 1883. Unlike the Greek text, this
version tells the moral first and then the story. The moral says, *Walk, even
slowly. Never be lazy when you go. And then you will reach a thousand miles
away.*

第一課 亀とうさぎ
　あゆむこと. おそしといへども. 怠らず. ゆくときは. つひに千里の遠き
にも. いたるべし. むかし兎と亀とありて. はしることをば. たくらべしが.
兎は. 己が足のはやきにほこり. 亀の歩みのおそきを侮りて. 途中に. ひと
ねぶりし. やがて目をさましてみれば. 亀は. はや定めたる処につきて. 勝
ちをとりしとぞ.

Why do you think the 1883 Japanese textbook writes the moral before
the episode, putting more emphasis on the moral of the story than on the entertainment? One reason for this modification may be that Japan's goal was
to catch up with Western countries in the late 19th century and used this story
for moral education suited to a new era. The Japanese educational tradition,
based on Confucianism,[7] highlighted discipline, while the 19th century Western education philosophy set value on the joy of learning, a concept foreign to
the Confucian style.[8]
　The children's song, "Usagi to Kame," made this fable well-loved in Japan. The song was introduced in *Yōnen Shōka Nihen, Jōkan*『幼年唱歌二編上
巻』in 1901, and since then it has been a Japanese favorite.

6　Nakatsukasa's source is *Augustanus Monacensis 564*, as cited in Perry's *Aesopica*. The
　most recent comprehensive translation from Greek is *Aesop's Fables* by Laura Gibbs.
　Gibbs translated "The Tortoise and the Hare" from Chambry's collection.
7　Confucianism is Jukyō 儒教 in Japanese.
8　Chapter 7 of *"Usagi to Kame" no Dokusho Bunkashi* by Fukawa Genichirō explains the
　details of moral education in Japanese elementary schools in the Meiji era.

もしもしカメよ　カメさんよ　せかいのうちで　おまえほど
あゆみののろい　ものはない　どうしてそんなに　のろいのか
　　　　　　　　　　　作詞：石原和三郎　　作曲：納所弁次郎

The 19ᵗʰ century British version

In Western countries during the 19ᵗʰ century, Aesop's fables were adapted and published in children's reading materials and textbooks. Thomas James's *Aesop's Fables* (1848) shows characteristics of the 19ᵗʰ century adaptation.

"The Hare and the Tortoise"

A hare once ridiculed the short feet and slow pace of the tortoise. But the tortoise laughed and replied, "Though you may be as swift as the wind, I'll beat you in the race." "All right," said the hare, "you'll soon live to regret those words."

So they agreed that the fox would choose the course and fix the goal. On the day appointed for the race, the tortoise started crawling at his usual steady pace without stopping a solitary moment. Of course, the hare soon left the tortoise far behind. Once he reached the midway mark, he began to nibble some juicy grass and amuse himself in different ways. Since the day was warm, he thought he would take a little nap in a shady

Figure 1 "**The Hare and the Tortoise**" [Illustration by Arthur Rackham, from Aesop's Fables, trans. V.S. Vernon Jones, 1912]

spot. Even if the tortoise might pass him while he slept, he was confident that he could easily overtake him again before he reached the goal. Meanwhile, the unwavering tortoise plodded on straight toward the goal. When the hare finally awoke, he was surprised to find that the tortoise was nowhere to be seen, and headed for the finish line as fast as he could. However, he dashed across the line only to see that the tortoise had crossed it before him and was comfortably resting and waiting for his arrival.

Moral: *Slow and steady wins the race.*

(Thomas James's 1848 version, cited in Zipes, *Aesop's Fables*)

What makes this version different from the Japanese school version? First, this is a very enjoyable story to read, with conversations of lively, human-like animals and descriptions of their behavior and thoughts. The elaborate and descriptive style implies that this is a written adaptation, because the style makes it more difficult to recite from memory. It also increases the reader's pleasure in imagining the details. Second, the moral is very short and placed at the end. Readers can enjoy the story first and then agree with the moral. Since the reader is able to think freely and interpret the story first, this placement of the moral is more effective and stimulating for children, I think, than the Japanese textbook method above. What do you think?

Another difference, and a very interesting one, is the fox, whom the tortoise and the hare ask to be a neutral judge of the race. The 19ᵗʰ century British versions were already popular when the Japanese textbook was written, and it is interesting that the Japanese textbook uses the simpler approach in spite of that fact. This probably suited the early Meiji era better, since the idea of judges in sporting competitions was new in Japan and might have been hard to understand. Vernacular literature has ample space to accept changes and variations to fit the culture of its readers.

African American version

African American people retold "The Tortoise and the Hare" with a surprising twist. The tortoise wins, of course, but the way he wins is different. There is an entertaining modern version, retold by Julius Lester, based on the traditional African American folk tale ("Old Hard Shell," Harris 86-90). In Lester's modern adaptation, the rabbit (hare) isn't lazy but hard working. He trains hard to prepare for the race. The turtle (tortoise), on the other hand, takes a totally different choice. His family get together to help him win.

> Brer Rabbit went into training. He bought a red jogging suit, a green sweatband, and some yellow Adidas sneakers, and he jogged ten miles every day. Then he'd come home and do a whole mess of push-ups, sit-ups, and skip rope to his records. Some folks wondered if he was training for a race or "Soul Train."[9]
> Brer Turtle didn't do a thing. You see, it's a strange thing about the Turtle family. There were six of 'em, including Brer Turtle, and they all looked alike. The only way to tell them apart was to put 'em under a magnifying glass, and even then you could make a mistake.
> ("Brer Rabbit Finally Gets Beaten," Lester 31–34)

On the day of the race, the six turtles get up early in the morning and place themselves one by one at each mile. Turtle's wife hides at the starting point. Each child stays at a milepost behind a bush. As for Brer Turtle him-

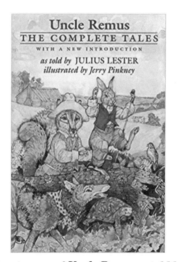

Figure 2   The front cover of *Uncle Remus*, retold by Julius Lester

---

9   "Soul Train" was a popular music-dance TV show in the United States from 1971 to 2006. The guests presented passionate dances with music. Many African American stars were featured in it. It was a long-running program that lasted for 35 years from 1971 to 2006.

self, he waits at the final post hiding in the woods. The race starts. The rabbit runs as fast as he can without rest. When the rabbit has nearly reached the first milepost, he calls for Brer Turtle, just to make sure of the distance between them. To the rabbit's surprise, the turtle (actually a turtle child) replies from the nearby bush. The upset rabbit runs even faster, yet a turtle is ahead of him every time. When the rabbit almost reaches the goal after a five-mile run, Brer Turtle appears from the woods and wins the race.

Are you surprised? The moral of this story certainly is not the value of diligence. The rabbit is hard-working but loses the race. The turtle cheats and wins. What does the story tell us? This African American version has its roots in "The Tortoise and the Falcon," a story from South Africa (Abrahams 75–77), in which the tortoise beats a falcon with the same trick. In both the African American version and the South African version, the tortoise is completely inferior in swiftness. In order to overcome this disadvantage, the tortoise relies on friendships, family ties, and trickery. "Use your brain, never fight alone" could be the moral of this version. Do you agree?

We can understand why African Americans support this particular plot if we know their history. The ancestors of African Americans were kidnapped from Africa and forced to work as slaves in America. They had no chance of "winning" in life while they were slaves. Even after the slavery era, through racial discrimination, African Americans have not been allowed an equal chance of success in society. Figuratively speaking, they have not had a fair chance in their race of life. In the Aesop story, the rabbit represents privileged people, for he is equipped with superior running ability. The turtle is doomed to lose if he runs the race following the rabbit's rules. He must have his own rules to win. The African American version, therefore, teaches you that you must outwit society in order to have an equal chance of victory.

Vernacular literature travels through the world and puts down its roots wherever it goes. Vernacular literature trips through time, too. The story of the tortoise and the hare was created in Greece over 2500 years ago and reached the American South. The story of the tortoise and the falcon traveled from Africa to America. The stories merged and became the African American version, which expresses different values. Vernacular literature is interesting because it is free to be reshaped and become your own work of literature.

4. Conclusion

"The Tortoise and the Hare" has been adapted in various media. It was adapted in a film in 1934 by the Walt Disney Company.[10] This film depicts the hare as a stereotypical frivolous playboy, but it also expresses the pleasure of life with brightly colored animation and joyful music. The hare is not harmed, and the victory of the tortoise is gaily celebrated. It is a happy film. There is also the Japanese song by Saitō Kazuyoshi, "Usagi to Kame."[11] The song is not targeted at children but rather at adults who are weary of working hard. It is a subdued parody of "The Tortoise and the Hare," saying nobody knows the goal but we all keep running on the track that someone unknown has set up for us. Saitō's song illustrates frustration in the competitive modern society.

Competition was the theme of "The Tortoise and the Hare" in the general understating of readers after the 19th century. The ancient interpretation, on the other hand, did not emphasize competition. (See the oldest text again, cited above.) Let me quote the ancient moral: *The story shows that many people have good natural abilities which are ruined by idleness; on the other hand, sobriety, zeal, and perseverance can prevail over indolence* (Gibbs 116).

Here you see that ancient Greeks were focused on self-cultivation by ceaseless effort. To them, the hare and tortoise represented two personalities: one seeks temporary pleasure, and the other steadily walks toward a goal. Aristotle (384–322 BCE), a Greek philosopher, taught that a person reaches the highest goodness only by constant mental effort. He also taught that the virtue of striving for the goal makes the person worthy and happy (Aristotle-Watanabe No. 5123). Both Aristotle and Aesop are speaking about what you do with yourself, not how you defeat others.

Vernacular literature reflects the values and life of the present society; as a text changes, its interpretation varies accordingly. It is amazing that we can read and appreciate a tale 2500 years after its creation. We can even learn life lessons from it. I would be delighted if you became interested in this field of study and explored the tremendous treasures of vernacular literature.

---

10 *The Tortoise and the Hare, in technicolor* (Walt Disney Productions, 1934) . https://www.youtube.com/watch?v=2DrKmpuKhKE, cited on February 20, 2021.

11 Kazuyoshi Saoto – Usagi to Kame [Music Video Short ver.] https://www.youtube.com/watch?v=WxX1JK-NQzA, cited on March 15, 2021.

References

Abrahams, Roger D., selected and retold by. *African Folktales*. Pantheon, 1983.

Gibbs, Laura, trans. by. *Aesop's Fables*. Oxford UP, 2002.

Harris, Joel Chandler. *The Favorite Uncle Remus*. Houghton Mifflin, 1948.

Lester, Julius. *The Tales of Uncle Remus: The Adventures of Brer Rabbit*. Dial, 1999.

Perry, Ben Edwin, ed. and trans. with commentary and historical essay. *Aesopica: A Series of Texts Relating to Aesop or Ascribed to Him or Closely Connected with the Literary Tradition that Bears His Name,* 3rd ed., U of Illinois P, 2007.

Zipes, Jack, ed. *Aesop's Fables*. Signet Classics, 1992.

イソップ／渡辺和雄訳『イソップ寓話集Ⅰ・Ⅱ』小学館，1982 年.

アリストテレス／渡辺邦夫・立花幸司訳『ニコマコス倫理 上』光文社古典新訳文庫，2015 年.

イソップ／中務哲郎訳『イソップ寓話集』岩波文庫，1999 年（Perry 版からギリシア語の 471 話を翻訳してある）.

原良策編『小学読本 初等科 巻四』1883 年.

納所弁次郎・田村虎蔵編『幼年唱歌 二編上巻』1901 年.

府川源一郎『「ウサギとカメ」の読書文化史：イソップ寓話の受容と「競争」』教勉出版，2017 年.

ローレンス・マルソー編・校註『絵入巻子本 伊曽保物語：翻刻・解題・図版解説』臨川書店，2021 年.

Further Reading

Borshuk, Michael. *Swinging the Vernacular: Jazz and African-American Modernist Literature*. Routledge, 2006.

Lemke, Sieglinde. *The Vernacular Matters of American Literature*. Palgrave McMillan, 2009.

日本語文献案内

　ヴァナキュラー文学は，民話，伝説，神話，歌，音楽，ファンタジー，ＳＦ，人間の心理などと深く関わっています．アニメ，漫画，ゲームなどのアイデアの源泉でもあります．知的関心を広げて取り組んでみましょう．

ウェルズ恵子編『ヴァナキュラー文化と現代社会』思文閣出版，2018 年.
ウェルズ恵子『魂をゆさぶる歌に出会う：アメリカ黒人文化のルーツへ』岩波ジュ

ニア新書，2014（第3刷2020）年.

浜田寿美男『私と他者と語りの世界：精神の生態学へ向けて』ミネルヴァ書房，
　　2009年.

アーシュラ・K. ル゠グウィン，青木由紀子訳『ファンタジーと言葉』岩波現代
　　文庫，2015年.

▋ 考えてみよう

1. 「ウサギとカメ」のバリエーションを, References にある資料から日本語版,
   英語版, アメリカ黒人の民話版で入手しましょう. それぞれ全文を原語で読
   み, 比較検討してください. 本書で触れてない相違点や類似点に気がつい
   たら, その意味を考えて分析し, 文章にしましょう.

2. あなたがよく知っている別の物語または歌詞のバリエーションを, 日本語と
   英語, または英語だけで, 最低3種類集めてください. それらを比較検討し,
   相違点と類似点について考察してください. どのような面白さ, 価値観, コ
   ミュニケーション機能をあなたは見出すでしょうか.

・・・

ウェルズ　恵子
Keiko WELLS

南アフリカの多言語主義と
12番目の公用語

Multilingual South Africa: Sign Language
Becomes the Twelfth Official Language

　アフリカは2000以上の言語が分布する多言語大陸です．各民族の言語，複数の民族が使用する地域共通語，さらにヨーロッパからの入植者や植民地政府がもたらしたヨーロッパ言語やそれが土着化して変化した言語などが複雑に絡み合い，併存してきました．家族とは母語である民族語で会話し，家を出てバスに乗ったら複数の言語を駆使しながら巧みにおしゃべりし，職場に到着すると英語やフランス語に切り替える——多くのアフリカ人がこのような多言語環境で暮らしています．

　なかでも南アフリカ共和国（以下南アフリカ）は，アフリカ大陸でも最多となる11もの公用語をもつ国です．[1] さらに近年では，手話（sign language）が12

図1　ヨハネスブルクにある憲法裁判所の正面玄関に設置された木製の扉には，権利章典に謳われた27の権利が11の公用語と手話で彫刻されている

1　11言語の内訳は，アフリカ系の9言語（ズールー語，コサ語，北ソト語，ソト語，スワジ語，南ンデベレ語，ツォンガ語，ツワナ語，ヴェンダ語），ヨーロッパ系の2言語（オランダ系移民の言語から派生したアフリカーンス語，英語）．

番目の公用語に認定される可能性が高まってきたことから，その独特の言語文化に注目が集まっています．

人種隔離体制の克服と若者たち

　南アフリカは多民族・多人種の国ですが，現在のような多言語主義に至るまでの道のりは平坦ではありませんでした．この地にはもともと狩猟採集や牧畜を行う人々が暮らしていましたが，4世紀頃より赤道地帯からの大規模な人の移動が起こり，現在の人口の約8割を占めるアフリカ人（Black Africans[2]）の祖先となっていきます．また，ヨーロッパ人による植民地化の歴史は17世紀にさかのぼります．まず1652年にオランダ東インド会社が現在のケープタウンに補給基地を建設，19世紀になるとイギリスからの入植と植民地建設が進みました．19世紀後半からはインドからの移民も到来します．そして，南アフリカ戦争（1899〜1902）を経て，1910年にイギリス帝国の自治領として南アフリカ連邦が成立します．人口の約2割（現在では1割弱）にすぎないヨーロッパ系住民が国土の大半を占有し，アフリカ人は残りの僻地に押し込められました．第二次世界大戦後，人種に基づく隔離の徹底を掲げる国民党が政権の座につくと，すべての国民を人種別に分類して「白人」以外の権利を抑制するアパルトヘイト体制が始動します．

　20世紀後半になると人種隔離に抵抗するアフリカ人の運動が広がりますが，その重要な契機となったのがソウェト蜂起（1976年）と呼ばれる事件です．国民党の主な支持者はオランダ語から派生したアフリカーンス語を母語とする人々だったことから，政府は教育言語の半分を英語，もう半分をアフリカーンス語とする方針を打ち出します．ヨハネスブルク郊外のソウェト地区では抑圧者の言語を押し付けられたことに反発した若者たちが抗議デモを展開，制圧しようとした警察隊が無差別に発砲したために多数の死傷者を出す惨事となります．数百人にのぼる死者のうち約3割が18歳以下というこの虐殺事件は国際社会にアパルトヘイト体制の残忍さを知らしめることになり，ひいてはこの国を民主化へと導く転換点となりました．

　1994年，初の全人種参加での総選挙を経てネルソン・マンデラが大統領に就

2　南アフリカの国勢調査では各人に所属する人種集団を尋ねており，2011年の調査結果では「Black African」が79.2%，「White」が8.9%，「Coloured」が8.9%，「Indian/Asian」が2.5%，その他が0.5%だった．このうち「Coloured」には，さまざまな組み合わせの異人種間通婚によって誕生した人びとと，オランダ東インド会社によって導入された奴隷の子孫，先住民で牧畜民の「コイ」，狩猟採集民の「サン」などが含まれる．

任，新憲法において11言語が公用語として承認されました．憲法内の権利章典では，人種，ジェンダー，性，妊娠，婚姻，民族的・社会的出自，肌の色，性的指向，年齢，障害，宗教，良心，信条，文化，言語，出生に基づくあらゆる差別が禁止されています．南アフリカの多言語主義は，過去の悲劇の産物であると同時に，どの言語で学ぶのかは自分たちで選択するという若者たちの誇りと熱意がもたらしたものなのです．

言語としての手話

　南アフリカの憲法第6条では，他の少数言語とともに，手話が「発展と使用を促進し，そのための条件を作り出す」義務を負う言語であると定められています．手話の普及に力を入れている国は多数ありますが，南アフリカでは1990年代より1つの言語として認知されているということ，少なくともそうなるべきだと考えられていることがわかります．

　手を使って会話をする人々がいたことはソクラテスの時代から記録されているそうですが，19世紀にヨーロッパで口話法が提唱されると手話の地位は低下し，克服すべき悪習のようにみなされるようになります．「障害者」を少しでも「健常者」に近づけることこそが教育の役割だと信じられていたということでしょう．西欧や日本において手話でのコミュニケーションが本格的に再評価されるのは，20世紀後半に入ってからのことです．

　これに対し，アフリカ各地では世界に先駆けて手話による教育事業が展開されるなど，手話は独特の地位を確立してきました．ヨーロッパ由来の口話法が導入されなかったこと，補聴器や人工内耳などの器具や医療技術へのアクセスが困難だったこともそれを後押ししたとみられます（亀井，2006）．その結果，聴こえない人々を聴覚の欠損といった側面からのみとらえるのではなく，手話という独自の文化を備えた集団とみなすような理解が生まれることになります．

　南アフリカでは，先に紹介した憲法に加え，南アフリカ学校法も手話を教育言語の1つとして定めてきました．さらに2017年には憲法審査会が手話を公用語として承認するよう提案を行い，公用語化への機運がいっそう高まっています．言語の多様性を尊重する土壌が，この国を世界でも指折りの手話先進国に押し上げたといえるでしょう．

▌文献案内

宮本正興・松田素二編『新書アフリカ史』改訂新版，講談社現代新書，2018年．
亀井伸孝『アフリカのろう者と手話の歴史：Ａ・Ｊ・フォスターの「王国」を訪

ねて』明石書店，2006 年.

▌英語で読んでみよう

　南アフリカを民主化に導いたネルソン・マンデラ元大統領が，南アフリカの憲法と差別の禁止について説明している部分です．読んでみましょう．

　　We in South Africa are celebrating a decade of non-racial, non-sexist, non-discriminatory democracy. (...) All of this stood in celebration of our democracy, based on the values of human dignity, the achievement of human equality and the advancement of human rights and freedoms. Under the equality clause in our constitution's bill of rights we affirm that, and I quote:

　　"The state may not unfairly discriminate directly or indirectly against anyone on one or more grounds, including race, gender, sex, pregnancy, marital status, ethnic or social origin, colour, sexual orientation, age, disability, religion, conscience, belief, culture, language and birth."

　　The constitution continues to affirm that no person may unfairly discriminate directly or indirectly against anyone on one or more of the grounds mentioned above.

　　We have striven to give legislative and regulatory content to these founding precepts in our nation-building constitution. We have in this past decade progressed, slow as it may have been, towards living together in the acknowledgement of the basic equality and right to dignity of all human beings.

　　(The Conference for the Disabled でのネルソン・マンデラによるスピーチ．2004 年 4 月 4 日)
　　http://db.nelsonmandela.org/speeches/pub_view.asp?pg=item&ItemID=NMS924&txtstr=human% 20rights

· ·

山本　めゆ
Meyu YAMAMOTO

アメリカ・人種差別・記念碑

Black Lives Matter and Confederate Symbols

概要

　この章では人種差別研究の一例として，アメリカ合衆国のブラック・ライヴズ・マター（BLM）運動と記念碑の問題を扱います．人種差別の根絶に異論の余地はなく，世界各地でさまざまな取組みが行われているのに，なぜ人種差別はなくならないのか．この単純とも思える問いに答えるために，人種差別研究はヘイトスピーチや暴力などの「見えやすい人種差別」だけではなく，既存の社会構造に組み込まれた「見えにくい人種差別」にも焦点を当てています．

　後者は「制度的人種差別」と呼ばれ，特に 2020 年の BLM 運動でその撤廃が訴えられたことで，あらためて注目を浴びました．その一例が記念碑です．記念碑がなぜ・どのように人種差別と関係するのか，という疑問への答えは，後半の英文の説明を読んで見つけてください．なお，英語の racism は厳密には「人種主義」と和訳されますが，この章では一般的によく使われる「人種差別」で統一します．

図1　コロナ禍の中で行われたフィラデルフィアの BLM デモ，2020 年 6 月
［Wikimedia Commons］

国際英語文化の中の人種差別研究

　2020年6月，拡大するBLM抗議デモの背景を解説した日本のニュース番組が，否定的なステレオタイプを助長する差別的な黒人像のアニメ動画をツイッターに掲載しました．動画は駐日米国臨時代理大使の「侮辱的で無神経」という投稿を含む多数の批判を受けて削除されたものの，すでに欧米の主要メディアで報道された後でした．番組内の解説についても，問題の核心である制度的人種差別の歴史に関する言及が一切なく，同時期の国際的な報道水準からかけ離れた内容であったことに，専門家から抗議と再発防止を求める声が上がりました．この出来事は，アメリカの人種差別という深刻な問題に対する日本の一部メディアの認識の欠如を物語ると同時に，それを国際社会に露呈することにもなりました．

　SNSの発達により，私たちは世界中の情報が瞬時に共有される時代を生きています．それは私たちの社会で起きていることが世界に瞬時に共有されることも意味します．英語が世界の共通語となった今，世界の人々とコミュニケーションをとるためには，これまで以上に国際標準の価値観を身につけなければなりません．日本を含む世界の人種差別の歴史を知ることは，そうした相互理解への第一歩なのです．

研究の大切さ

　人種差別の問題を研究することの大切さを疑う読者は誰もいないでしょう．しかし，この章がトピックとする記念碑までもが研究対象になると聞くと，疑問に思う人もいるかもしれません．この研究の大切さは，ディズニーのキャラクターや商品ロゴ，辞書の例文など，一見すると人種差別とは無関係とも思われる文化事象とその背景を扱うことにもあります．

　「アフリカ文学の父」とも呼ばれるナイジェリア出身の作家チヌア・アチェベ（1930-2013）は，あるインタビューでアフリカのことわざを紹介したことがあります．それは，「ライオンたちが自分たち自身の歴史家を持つまでは，狩りの歴史はつねに猟師を讃えるだろう (Until the lions have their own historians, the history of the hunt will always glorify the hunter.)」というものです．「勝者の歴史」という言葉があるように，歴史として記録されてきたことだけが過去の出来事のすべてを伝えているわけではありません．ライオンのように殺される側，虐げられ声を奪われてきた側の物語を知ることなしに，過去の全貌をとらえることはできないのです．

　人種差別研究，特に見えにくい制度的人種差別の研究は，こうした声なき声を掘り起こし，見えなくされてきたものを見えるようにする作業でもあります．

この章のトピック

　この章では人種差別研究の例として，アメリカの記念碑の問題について考えます．具体的に取り上げるのは，南部連合のさまざまなシンボルです．

　南部連合の正式名称はアメリカ連合国．建国前17世紀半ばに奴隷制が確立したアメリカでは，やがて奴隷制を廃止した北部の州と奴隷制を継続・擁護した南部の州の間で，何度も対立が起こります．そうした中，1860年の大統領選挙で奴隷制の拡大に反対するエイブラハム・リンカンが当選したことから，南部の11州がアメリカ合衆国（連邦）を脱退し，アメリカ連合国（南部連合）を結成したのです．南北戦争と呼ばれる内戦が勃発し，4年間続いた戦争は北軍の勝利で終わります．南部連合は再び連邦に統一され，奴隷制は廃止されました．

　南部連合のシンボルとは，南北戦争で戦い敗れた南軍の兵士や指揮官を顕彰するものです．銅像や銘板などの記念碑だけではなく，祝日や記念日，軍旗，さらにはロバート・E・リー将軍やジェファソン・デイヴィス連合国大統領などの名前を冠した施設（学校，道路，米軍基地，公園，橋，ダムなど）も含みます．

　南部貧困法律センターという人権団体の2016年の報告書によると，古戦場や墓地などのゆかりの地に建つ記念碑を除き，全米には1500以上の南部連合のシンボルが存在し，その多くが元南部連合の州にありました．設立された時期や場所を歴史的に分析すると，南部連合のシンボルは単に過去の出来事を記憶するためではなく，人種隔離制度という奴隷制廃止後の白人至上主義的な社会構造を維持・強化するために設置されたことがわかるのです．

　南部連合のシンボルに対しては何度も撤去や施設名変更の声が上がりましたが，2020年のBLM運動での訴えは最多の銅像撤去や改称へと結実しました．「黒人の命は大切だ」とも訳されるBLMは，多発する警官による黒人殺害事件（＝見えやすい人種差別）に抗議しただけではなく，コロナ禍で浮き彫りになったさまざまな格差や不平等（＝見えにくい人種差別・制度的人種差別）をも問題視し，撤廃を訴えました．その中で記念碑も抗議の対象となったのです．南部連合のシンボルは，アメリカの制度的人種差別の起源たる奴隷制を擁護するために戦った人々を讃えるもので，いわば人種差別の文化的遺産でした．それらが今でも全米の公共空間に存在し続けていることの問題を，BLMは鋭く指摘しました．人種差別研究は，現代の諸問題を理解するための歴史的視座を提供してくれるのです．

研究の素材

　人種差別研究では，研究対象を見えやすい人種差別とするのか，見えにくいものとするのかで，扱う素材が大きく異なります．もちろん，どの時代の事象に着目するかによってもさまざまでしょう．前者ならば，奴隷制下で虐げられた黒人たちの体験を，わずかながら刊行された手記や，1930年代に行われた聞き取り調査の音源・書き起こし資料，さらに奴隷制末期の写真などから紐解くことができるかもしれません．あるいは，過去に起こった人種暴力致死事件を，新聞記事やその他の歴史資料（史料）から明らかにすることもできるでしょう．人権団体や社会運動家が活動の記録を残している場合も多いので，そうした史料が見つかれば，研究にさらなる厚みが加わります．

　かつてこれらの史料を閲覧収集するためには，全米各地の史料館や大学図書館に調査に行くことが不可欠でしたが，今では数多くの史料がデジタル化され，どこからでもアクセスできます．ただし，実物を目にすることができる現地での史料調査は，画面上からは感じ取れない歴史のアクチュアリティを感じられる貴重な機会でもあります．

　他方，後者の見えにくい人種差別（＝制度的人種差別）の場合は，この章で取り上げる記念碑のように，一見すると人種差別とは無関係のように思われる素材が対象となることが多々あります．したがって，常識にとらわれることなく研究対象を探し当てることが大切です．また，例えばBLM運動が批判する現代の刑事司法制度における人種差別や医療・所得・教育の人種格差，住宅差別などの問題を扱う場合，その原因となった当時の政策や法律を検討することがあるかもしれません．しかし政策決定過程を記した議会文書や法律文には，人種差別を意図するようなあからさまな議論や特定の人種・エスニック集団を名指しするような文言は通常出てこないため，その他の関連データや史資料を総合的に判断し，書かれていないことをあぶり出す批判的分析力も必要です．

研究がめざすこと

　3章でも述べられているとおり，学術研究は「当たり前とされていることに疑いをもつ」ことが出発点となります．例えば，この章で扱う南部連合の記念碑は，あまりにもアメリカの日常に溶け込んでいて，当たり前の風景になっているかもしれません．しかし実際には，これらのシンボルは既存の社会構造を維持強化するために建てられたことが，この章の考察で明らかになります．

　また，白人男性を讃える多数のシンボルが長い間アメリカの公共空間を支配してきた一方で，黒人や先住民，アジア系，ヒスパニック系といった人種・エスニックマイノリティの経験を記念するシンボルがほとんどないこと——つまり景観に隠された人種不平等や格差の問題にも，この研究は気づかせてくれます．女性や性的マイノリティのシンボルも同様に少ないので，景観における構造的な性差別の問題へと研究の射程を広げることもできます．

　人種差別はしばしば個人的な偏見や心の問題だと言われます．専門家でさえ，そのように解説することもあるほどです．しかし，いくら個人が「差別はやめよう」と心がけても一向に人種差別がなくならないのは，長い時間をかけて社会構造の中に組み込まれた不平等が人々の目には見えなくなっていたり，その社会構造から恩恵を受ける側にいるために，人々がそれを見ようとはせず，結果として人種差別に加担していたりするからです．

　こうした社会構造を抜本的に変革することなしに，人種差別を根絶することはできません．人種差別研究は，その見えにくい仕組みを歴史的に詳らかにすることで，抜本的な社会変革への道筋を提供しているのです．

Black Lives Matter and Confederate Symbols

TABLE OF CONTENTS

1.　Introduction

　No one would disagree that we must eliminate racism, because it is wrong to discriminate against someone based on race. Given that, why does racism continue to exist everywhere? To answer this question, the study of racism focuses not only on "overt racism" such as hate speech and racial violence but also on "covert racism" that has been built in the existing social structure. It is particularly important to examine the latter, because this hidden form of racism, called *institutional racism*, is hard to see and therefore difficult to eliminate. The Black Lives Matter movement has tried to shed light on both overt and covert racism in various ways, which will be a topic of this chapter.

2. Black Lives Matter and Confederate Symbols

In the early summer of 2020, the protest movement called "Black Lives Matter" (hereafter BLM) drew public attention worldwide to the problem of police brutality and institutional racism in the United States. There were various efforts to correct legacies of this long-standing problem. Among such efforts was the removal of flags, facility names and statues of war "heroes," all associated with the Confederate States of America (hereafter the Confederacy).

The Confederacy was a coalition of eleven states in the American South that seceded from the United States after the election of President Abraham Lincoln in 1860 and fought to maintain slavery during the Civil War (1861–1865). While it was never recognized as an independent nation, the Confederacy elected its own president and vice president, and created its own constitution, flags and anthems. Today, the flag that was used on battlefields during the Civil War is generally called the Confederate battle flag, and is often considered as a symbol of racism. The BLM movement was a catalyst to banning the display of the Confederate battle flag at the NASCAR car races and on the U.S. military bases.

President Donald J. Trump repeatedly opposed the removal of these Confederate symbols. When asked on a TV interview whether the Confederate flag was offensive, he answered as follows: "It depends on who you're talking

Figure 1   The Confederate battle flag [Wikimedia Commons]

about, when you're talking about. When people —when people proudly have their Confederate flags, they're not talking about racism. They love their flag, it represents the South, they like the South."[1]

It is often argued that Confederate symbols have nothing to do with racism but rather are simply praising the heritage and regional pride of the South. But if they merely symbolize Southern heritage, why do BLM protesters see these symbols as problematic enough to be removed? What kind of Southern heritage do they represent? What were the stories behind these symbols? To answer these questions, this chapter focuses on the BLM movement and the problem of Confederate symbols. After giving a brief overview of BLM, the chapter considers when and how these symbols appeared.

3. What is Black Lives Matter?

The phrase "Black Lives Matter" was created in 2013 by three Black women (two of whom define themselves as queer) community activists: Alicia Garza, Patrisse Cullors and Opal Tometi. It stems from the 2012 fatal shooting of a Black high school student named Trayvon Martin by a member of the neighborhood watch in Sanford, Florida. The killer was found not guilty of a crime in 2013. Upon hearing news of this verdict, Garza posted on her Facebook a comment with the phrase "Black Lives Matter." Cullors saw it and shared the hashtag #blacklivesmatter, which went viral on SNS. The phrase BLM became the name of the movement in 2014 when protest demonstrations took place in Ferguson, Missouri, after another Black teenager, Michael Brown, was shot to death by white police.[2]

In 2013, they created an online community platform named the Black Lives Matter Global Network (hereafter BLMGN). Since then, the group has hosted discussions about anti-racism and promoted community organizing. One of the characteristics of the BLMGN is that it focuses on experiences of women, LGBTQ, and other marginalized people. This is because Black liberation movements in the past, such as the Civil Rights movement and the Black Power movement, were led by heterosexual, cisgender men, who, according to BLM founders, kept others in the background of the movements. BLMGN's

---

1 "Transcript: 'Fox News Sunday' Interview with President Trump," *Fox News* online, July 19, 2020, https://www.foxnews.com/politics/transcript-fox-news-sunday-interview-with-president-trump.

2 BLMGN, "8 Years Strong," July 13, 2021, https://blacklivesmatter.com/8-years-strong/.

56

support for all Black lives also comes out of an awareness that when protests occur, the focus tends to fall on incidents in which Black men are the victims.[3]

BLMGN defines BLM as follows: "Black Lives Matter is an ideological and political intervention in a world where Black lives are systematically and intentionally targeted for demise. It is an affirmation of Black folks' humanity, our contributions to this society, and our resilience in the face of deadly oppression."[4] Not only does "Black" include all Black people; "Lives" also means all the rights to live a safe, civic human life. These messages are written on the "Herstory" page of the BLMGN website. This newer term, *herstory*, merits further attention. Given that the word "history" appears to consist of "his" and "story," the BLMGN deliberately uses "herstory" as a play on words to emphasize that stories of all women—straight, queer, trans, and nonbinary—should also be told.

Compared to the BLM protests of 2014, the 2020 BLM demonstrations are unique in terms of its scope and duration, as well as the diversity of its participants. The immediate trigger of the 2020 protests was the killing of George Floyd, a Black man who was murdered by a white police officer in Minneapolis, Minnesota on May 25. However, just as was the case in 2014, before and after this incident a number of Black men, women and transgender people were killed as a result of police brutality and other racially motivated violence. According to the *New York Times*, BLM protests took place in more than 2,000 locations across the United States just in the first two weeks after the murder of Floyd. Demonstrations and marches were held in every state and Washington D.C. Not only large cities but also small towns that had never experienced such protests before became home to the BLM movement.[5]

While the BLM movement is often called the second Civil Rights movement, one unique characteristic is its lack of central leaders, in contrast with the original Civil Rights movement with its famous leaders like Martin Luther King, Jr. In fact, BLM considers itself a leader*ful*, rather than leader*less*, movement, where anyone can become a leader. BLM intentionally takes this style partly because they believe that movements that depend on a few promi-

3   BLMGN, "Herstory," accessed August 8, 2021. https://blacklivesmatter.com/herstory/.
4   *Ibid.*
5   Audra D. S. Burch, et al., "How Black Lives Matter Reached Every Corner of America," *New York Times* online, June 13, 2020, https://www.nytimes.com/interactive/2020/06/13/us/george-floyd-protests-cities-photos.html.

nent leaders become unsustainable without them. Greater diversity in participants' age, sexual orientation/gender identity and racial/ethnic background is an important point of development in BLM compared to 2014. Equally important is that in 2020 BLM demonstrations spread to many places around the world, including Japan, where protest marches were held in such places as Tokyo, Nagoya, Osaka, Kyoto, Fukuoka and Okinawa.

Although the BLM constituencies of 2014 and 2020 are different in many ways, the central message has remained the same from the beginning: eliminating *institutional racism*. Institutional racism, also known as structural racism or systemic racism, is a form of racism that is embedded within society as normal practice. In the United States, it stems from the institution of slavery, where Black people were unfairly treated and exploited as slaves. Even after the abolition of slavery as a result of the Civil War, discrimination against Blacks continued in employment, housing, education, healthcare and criminal justice, to name only a few domains.

To solve these persisting problems of institutional racism, swift changes or signs of changes surfaced during the 2020 BLM activism. For example, in response to BLM's "Defund the Police" rallying cry, some cities came up with a plan to reinvest the budget for the criminal justice system into healthcare and education for communities in need. New York City announced that it would shift about $1 billion from NY Police Department's budget to youth and social services programming.[6]

Moreover, Disneyland Park in California and Magic Kingdom Park in Florida decided to retire one of their most popular theme park rides, Splash Mountain. This was because the theme of this ride was based on the old musical film *Song of the South* (1946), which had long been criticized for its racist songs and negative portrayal of Black people. Many scholars have pointed out that these stereotypes helped maintain institutional racism in the United States. Disney replaced Splash Mountain with a new ride inspired by *Princess and the Frog* (2009), the first Disney Princess film featuring a Black heroine.[7]

6　Kristina Sgueglia and Scottie Andrew, "New York Police Department's Budget Has Been Slashed by $1 Billion," *CNN* online, July 1, 2020, https://edition.cnn.com/2020/07/01/us/new-york-budget-nypd-1-billion-cut-trnd/index.html.

7　Brooks Barnes, "Disney's Splash Mountain to Drop 'Song of the South' Depictions," *New York Times* online, June 25, 2020, https://www.nytimes.com/2020/06/25/business/media/disney-splash-mountain-princess-frog.html.

Another change was the state flag of Mississippi, which had included in its design the Confederate battle flag since 1894. BLM protesters called for change in its design, and in late June of 2020, the Mississippi State Legislature passed a bill that would remove the flag from public buildings and design a new flag. In September, the new flag design was chosen to put on the general election ballot in November as the 2020 Mississippi flag referendum. The referendum asked Mississippi voters whether the new design should be adopted as the new official state flag. It was approved by a large margin of 73% to 27%.[8]

Finally, Confederate statues and flags were removed as mentioned in the introduction. According to *NBC News*, as of late September 2020 more than 130 statues had already been removed.[9] Further, there were actions by cities and states to change the names of buildings, schools, streets and the like, which were named after people who supported slavery or racism. A federal law established a commission to rename military bases, ships and other assets named for Confederate leaders.

4. The Problem of Confederate Symbols

In 2016, the Southern Poverty Law Center (hereafter SPLC), one of the most well-known U.S. human rights organizations, published a study report entitled *Whose Heritage?: Public Symbols of the Confederacy*. The study collected information on Confederate symbols in public spaces across the United States. It listed these symbols in chronological order and created a distribution map.

The study was a direct response to a horrific incident called the Charleston massacre. In 2015, a 21-year-old white supremacist attended a Bible study at a Black church in Charleston, South Carolina, and murdered nine Black people who welcomed him. The pictures of him holding the Confederate battle flag, which appeared in the media after this shocking mass shooting, ignited a nationwide movement to remove the flag and other Confederate

---

8   Emily Wagster Pettus, "Mississippi's New Magnolia Flag Starting to Fly after Vote," *AP News* online, November 5, 2020, https://apnews.com/article/election-2020-religion-race-and-ethnicity-mississippi-elections-3e31d01e0e0b8c062ea202b7d8424ecf.

9   Erik Ortiz, "These Confederate Statues Were Removed. But Where Did They Go?," *NBC News* online, September 20, 2020, https://www.nbcnews.com/news/us-news/these-confederate-statues-were-removed-where-did-they-go-n1240268.

symbols from public spaces.[10]

While it became clear that many local governments across the South honored legacies of the Confederacy in some way, the exact number of publicly supported Confederate symbols remained unknown. That is why the SPLC conducted this study. The Confederate symbols catalogued by the SPLC include monuments and statues; flags; holidays and other observances; and the names of schools, highways, parks, bridges, counties, cities, lakes, dams, roads, military bases, and other public places.[11]

The study found that there were more than 1,500 Confederate symbols in public spaces across the United States. About a half of them were Confederate statues and monuments. The SPLC excluded about 2,500 symbols, such as Civil War battlefields, markers, cemeteries and others, which simply reflect historical events. Rather than focusing on these symbols that belonged to their expected places, the SPLC paid particular attention to Confederate symbols found in unexpected places that had nothing to do with their historical contexts. Other findings (as of 2016) were as follows:

- The top ten states that have the most symbols are all former Confederate states.

- There are more than one hundred public schools named after prominent Confederate leaders such as Robert E. Lee. Most of them are in the former Confederate states. About a third of these schools have student populations that are majority Black.

- Although South Carolina and Alabama removed the Confederate battle flag from their capitol grounds after the Charleston massacre, six former Confederate states, including Mississippi, Florida and Texas still allow it to fly in public places.

---

10 Southern Poverty Law Center (SPLC), *Whose Heritage?: Public Symbols of the Confederacy* (Southern Poverty Law Center, 2016), 6-7, https://www.splcenter.org/sites/default/files/com_whose_heritage.pdf. The updated version of this study became available on February 1, 2019. https://www.splcenter.org/20190201/whose-heritage-public-symbols-confederacy#methodology.

11 *Ibid.*, 9-10.

• There are ten major U.S. military bases named in honor of Confederate military leaders. All of them are located in the former Confederate states of Alabama, Georgia, Louisiana, North Carolina, Texas and Virginia.[12]

It is important to note that these Confederate symbols appeared not immediately after the Civil War, but long after the war. According to the SPLC report, there were two boom periods of construction. The first took place between the 1900s and the 1920s, when Blacks, freed from slavery and granted citizenship and voting rights, faced racial segregation, disenfranchisement, and illegal racial violence called lynching. It was also during these years that the white supremacist group called the Ku Klux Klan (KKK) was on revival.[13]

Confederate symbols emerged during this period when Black lives were suppressed to preserve white political and social supremacy. For example, in 1927 when the unveiling ceremony of the statue of Confederate President Jefferson Davis was held at a national military park in Mississippi, the former U.S. Senator John Williams made the following speech:

> The cause of White Racial Supremacy ... is not a "Lost Cause." It is a Cause Triumphant. ... The white man's family life, his code of social ethics, his racial integrity—in a word his civilization—the destruction of which in the slave states was dreaded, as the involved racial result of the abolition of slavery without deportation, are safe. All the dire results ... have been avoided by us.[14]

To Williams, "all the dire results" meant Blacks gaining equality to whites. He affirmed to his (probably all white) audience that these results were "avoided by us" to keep white civilization safe. For this purpose, they used such tactics as segregation, disenfranchisement and lynching. In Mississippi,

---

12 *Ibid.*, 10–12.
13 *Ibid.*, 14.
14 *The Jefferson Davis Memorial in the Vicksburg National Memorial Park* (Vicksburg, MS: Jefferson Davis Memorial Commission, 1927), 18, https://archive.org/details/TheJeffersonDavisMemorialInTheVicksburgNationalMilitaryPark.

Figure 2　The statue of a Confederate soldier (erected in 1913) on the courthouse
ground in Sumner, Mississippi [Photo taken by the author]

nearly 300 Blacks were lynched between the 1900s and the 1920s.[15]

Also notable is that most of Confederate statues and monuments during this period were built on government office grounds—particularly on courthouse grounds.[16]

Why courthouse grounds? At that time, whites often lynched Blacks on a courthouse lawn or hung the lynched body to a courthouse tree to warn other Blacks to stay in their place. They intentionally chose this location to show off that their version of justice was accomplished. (Recall Senator William's remark that the cause of white supremacy was a cause triumphant.) In a similar sense, erecting Confederate symbols on courthouse grounds may have been a sign sent by racist whites to show their intention to rule the local judiciary.

The second boom came between the mid-1950s and the late 1960s, when the Civil Rights movement was taking place. Although it was shorter and smaller in scale than the first period, one distinct characteristic is that many schools were renamed after Confederate leaders during this period. These school name changes occurred immediately after the historic decision of the U.S. Supreme Court called *Brown v. Board of Education* (1954), which ruled

---

15　Julius E. Thompson, *Lynchings in Mississippi: A History, 1865-1965* (Jefferson, NC: McFarland, 2006), 48, 65, 83.

16　SPLC, *Whose Heritage?*, 14-15.

that racial segregation in public schools were unconstitutional.[17]

The renamed schools sent a clear message that they were against this decision. That is, to oppose desegregation that would weaken the existent social structure of racial segregation in the South, these schools intentionally renamed themselves in honor of Confederate leaders who symbolized white supremacy. At the same time, Black children and students who attended racially desegregated schools faced frequent resentment and harassment from whites. In 1962, for example, hundreds of white students at the University of Mississippi protested their school's decision to enroll its first Black student. Some were waving the Confederate battle flag during the protest.[18]

5. Conclusion

As seen above, most Confederate symbols emerged in the postbellum Southern landscape with a clear purpose and timing of keeping the contemporary racial hierarchy. Confederate symbols functioned to maintain and reinforce the white supremacist power structure from the post-slavery era to the Civil Rights era, just as the stereotypical images of Black people were created to justify institutional racism of each time. Stereotypes and symbols that we see now have been a major factor in sustaining this system to this day.

In his *Mainichi Shimbun* interview on the removal of statues, American Studies scholar Yujin Yaguchi has pointed out that while the dynamics of discrimination have permeated the landscape, such everyday scenery seems so natural that no one questions if it is problematic.[19] This is precisely what BLM protestors questioned in 2020. They drew our attention to the problem that symbols honoring legacies of white men had long dominated public spaces in the United States and excluded other symbols remembering people of color, women, LGBTQ, and so on. BLM challenged such inequalities hidden in the landscape.

In this way, BLM's effort to eliminate legacies of institutional racism was not limited to legal and political reforms. Because cultural reforms are perhaps the most familiar area for many people, the removal of Confederate symbols was an equally important step forward to radically change the racial and

---

17 *Ibid.*, 15.

18 Equal Justice Initiative, *Segregation in America* (Equal Justice Initiative, 2018), 39.

19 *Mainichi Shimbun*, June 26, 2020, https://mainichi.jp/articles/20200626/k00/00m/030/121000c.

social structure of the United States.

References

AP News. November 5, 2020.

Black Lives Matter Global Network. https://blacklivesmatter.com/.

CNN. July 1, 2020.

Coates, Ta-Nehisi. *We Were Eight Years in Power: An American Tragedy*. New York: Random House, 2017.

Equal Justice Initiative. *Segregation in America*. Montgomery: Equal Justice Initiative, 2018.

Fox News. July 19, 2020.

Garza, Alicia. *The Purpose of Power: How We Come Together When We Fall Apart*. New York: Random House, 2020.

The Jefferson Davis Memorial in the Vicksburg National Memorial Park. Vicksburg, MS: Jefferson Davis Memorial Commission, 1927.

Mainichi Shimbun. June 26, 2020.

NBC News. September 20, 2020.

The New York Times. June 25 and July 13, 2020.

Southern Poverty Law Center. *Whose Heritage?: Public Symbols of the Confederacy*. Southern Poverty Law Center, 2016. https://www.splcenter.org/sites/default/files/com_whose_heritage.pdf.

Taylor, Keeanga-Yamahtta. *From #BlackLivesMatter to Black Liberation*. Chicago: Haymarket Books, 2016.

Thompson, Julius E. *Lynchings in Mississippi: A History, 1865–1965*. Jefferson, NC: McFarland, 2006.

Williams, Chad, Kidada E. Williams, and Keisha N. Blain, eds. *Charleston Syllabus: Readings on Race, Racism, and Racial Violence*. Athens: University of Georgia Press, 2016.

Further Reading

Savage, Kirk. *Standing Soldiers, Kneeling Slaves: Race, War, and Monument in Nineteenth-Century America*. Princeton: Princeton University Press, 1997.

Berkowitz, Bonnie, and Adrian Blanco. "Confederate Monuments Are Falling, but Hundreds Still Stand. Here's Where." *Washington Post* online, July 2, 2020. https://www.washingtonpost.com/graphics/2020/national/confederate-monuments/.

日本語文献案内

坂下史子「人種的〈他者〉としての黒人性—アメリカの人種ステレオタイプを例に」兼子歩・貴堂嘉之編『「ヘイト」の時代のアメリカ史：人種・民族・国籍を考える』彩流社，2017年.

「総特集 ブラック・ライヴズ・マター」『現代思想』10月臨時増刊号，第48巻第13号，青土社，2020年.

考えてみよう

1.　2020年のBLM運動では，警察暴力だけではなく，黒人の新型コロナ感染率・死亡率が白人の倍以上だったことにも抗議の声が上がりました．この人種格差の要因は何でしょうか？　アメリカ社会の中で常態化し，見えにくくなっている差別構造（＝制度的人種差別）について，具体的に考えてみましょう.

2.　日本における景観の「常識」（当たり前のように感じられる風景）についても考えてみましょう．例えば，みなさんの学校に銅像や記念碑，誰かの名前を冠した建物はありますか？　そこには何らかの不平等の力学が見出せるでしょうか？　これらのシンボルのデザインも分析してみましょう.

・・

坂下　史子
Fumiko SAKASHITA

5

アメリカ・性差別・男性フェミニスト
The #MeToo Movement and Male Feminists

概要

　この章ではフェミニズム研究の一例として，アメリカの #MeToo 運動について考察します．#MeToo 運動の争点である性的暴行の主たる被害者は言うまでもなく女性です．当事者性という点で，加害者側である男性の性別カテゴリーに属する筆者に，女性やフェミニズムについて語る資格があるのか疑問に思う読者がいるかもしれません．しかし，男性がこれまで女性主体で語られてきた性差別問題について考え，フェミニズムと真摯に向き合うことは，ジェンダー平等社会を作っていく上で重要なことなのです．#MeToo 運動を男性の視点からとらえ直すことは，これからの国際社会の枠組みの中で男女が手を取り合い，どのように社会に根づくジェンダー規範[1] を変えてゆくかについて考えるきっかけとなるはずです．

Figure 1　2018 年 1 月、米メリーランド州ボルチモアで
行われた女性集会 [Wikimedia Commons]

1　ジェンダー規範は，男性なら男らしく，女性なら女らしく振る舞うべき，といった男女のあり方を固定化する考えのことを指します．

国際英語文化の中のフェミニズム研究

2017年10月5日，ハリウッドの映画プロデューサーによる性的暴行に関する記事がニューヨーク・タイムズで公表されたことを起点に，性的被害を受けた女性たちがTwitter上で「私も（"me too"）」と呼びかけたことで #MeToo 運動は始まりました．以後，女性たちを中心に展開されたこのフェミニズム運動は，男性ロックミュージシャンによる性的暴行の告発や，ミスユニバースのあり方に対する賛否両論など，SNSを中心に多様な様相を呈することになります．#MeToo 運動により，世界中の人々がSNSを通じて女性に対する性的暴行に対する問題意識を共有する機会を得たのです．

これまでフェミニズム研究は，国際的視野のもと世界中の女性が直面するさまざまな問題について取り上げ，解決の糸口を模索してきました．この研究は特に，女性の経験や体験を誰もがわかる形に言語化・理論化し，伝達可能な共有知識として発展させることをめざしてきました．#MeToo 運動では，SNSを通じて，また，英語という国際共通言語を通じて，女性の性的被害経験が実直な言葉をもって世界中の人々に発信され，多くの共感を得るに至っています．そして，この運動の根幹に，個人の問題を全体の問題としてとらえ，伝達可能な共有知識として広めることの重要性を唱えたフェミニズム研究の貢献があることを忘れてはなりません．SNSの広がりによってフェミニズム研究は，性別，人種，言語，国籍を超えた多様性を包摂する学問としての発展を遂げようとしているのです．

研究の大切さ

フェミニズムは決して女性のためだけの学問ではなく，その担い手は性別，人種，国籍を例にとっても多種多様です．この研究において重要なことは，お節介なまでに他人の問題に首を突っ込むことです．他人の抱える問題に目を向けることで，それが実は自分にとって無関係な問題ではないことに気づく機会となるかもしれないのです．#MeToo 運動は，SNS上で発信される個人の問題に首を突っ込んでみたいと思った人が増えたことで拡大した運動でもあるのです．

筆者を含め，男性が女性主体で展開される #MeToo 運動について積極的に自己の見解を発信することは，しばしば当事者性論争を巻き起こします．ちなみに，当事者性にあたる明確な訳語が英語にはないため，後の英文説明では自分の立ち位置を意味する「positionality」という語を使っています．話を戻しますが，読者のなかには男性のことは男性が，女性のことは女性がよくわかっている，といっ

た考え方こそが当事者性であると考える人が少なからずいるのではないでしょうか．相手が同性であろうと異性であろうと，自分以外の人間を理解することは容易なことではありません．自分と他人がそれぞれに問題を抱え，それを SNS 上で口に出して伝え合うことで，「この人はそういう問題を抱えているんだ」と認識し共感することができます．他人の問題に触発され自分の問題に向き合ってみようと思う意志が生まれる，これこそがフェミニズム研究における当事者性なのかもしれません．

この章のトピック

　この章ではフェミニズム研究の一例として，#MeToo 運動の発端とされるアメリカの映画産業の中心であるハリウッドが抱える性的暴行問題を出発点に，女性と男性が今後どのようにフェミニズムと関わっていくべきかについて考えます．主に取り上げるのは，#MeToo 運動に対する男性側の反応です．被害者である女性側の訴えは想像にたやすい一方，当事者ではない男性側の声は正と負に分かれる傾向にあります．彼らの声に耳を傾けることを通してこの運動の今後のあり方を共に考えていきましょう．

　女性に対する性的暴行問題を扱う上で，前述した声という記録以外に，ジェンダー用語についても注目する必要があります．#MeToo 運動以降，男性を否定的にとらえることを目的にさまざまなジェンダー用語が使われるようになります．例えば，man（男性）と explaining（説明する）からなる造語で，男性が女性を上から目線で説教することを意味する「mansplaining（マンスプレイニング）」という言葉があり，2018 年にはオックスフォード英語辞典にも掲載されています．このようなジェンダー用語に対する見識を深めることは大変重要なことであり，それは時として研究素材の脆弱な部分を補う言語的な手助けになるかもしれません．

研究の素材

　フェミニズム研究で扱う研究素材は，公文書，歴史書，小説，詩，歌，映画，アニメーション，音楽，その他の芸術作品，コマーシャル，広告，雑誌，新聞記事，日記，書簡，フィールドワーク（参与観察）で得られる取材記録や統計データなど多岐にわたります．なかには，言語，ファッション，仕草や振る舞いといった人間のパフォーマティブな特性そのものが研究素材になることもあります．本

章では，#MeToo 運動に関わった人々の声という参与観察から得られる記録を研究素材として扱います．

　繰り返しになりますが，フェミニズム研究は個人の経験や体験を研究素材として用い，それらを誰もがわかる形に言語化・理論化し，伝達可能な共有知識として発展させることをめざします．アメリカの第二波フェミニズム運動[2]のスローガン「個人的なことは政治的である（The personal is political）」が示唆する通り，#MeToo 運動における個人の経験が政治性を帯び，誰もが理解できる形に言語化され，伝達可能な共有知識として認識されるとき，それは立派な研究素材となるのではないでしょうか．素材研究で重要なことは，さまざまな素材を臨機応変に多角的に取り込み分析し，解釈の過程で釈然としない状況に直面したとき，それを打破するために必要な新たな素材（知識）を探す（養う）気力，その源流である無限の好奇心をもち続けることではないかと思います．

研究がめざすこと

　#MeToo 運動の発祥地であり，ジェンダー平等社会として日本よりもはるかにダイバーシティの根づいたアメリカ社会においても，依然として男尊女卑の社会通念は根強く残っています．しかし，#MeToo 運動を機に全米各地では，#IHave や #HowIWillChange など，これまで女性を性的搾取の対象として扱ってきた加害者側の男性たちによる，自らの女性差別体験の告白や反省，行動変容に対する強い意志表明を主たる目的とするハッシュタグ・アクティビズム[3]が広がりを見せています．

　男性側がいかなる弁解をしようとも，女性に対する性的暴行の事実が揺らぐことは決してありません．しかし，すべての男性が女性の敵なのでもありません．女性たちの抱える問題に関心をもち，共にジェンダー平等な社会を模索しようとする男性をプロ（親）フェミニストと呼びます．彼らの多くは，伝統的な男らしさや仕事一辺倒なライフスタイルを拒否し，自分らしく生きる方法をフェミニズムの中に求めています．逆に，女性のなかにはフェミニズムや女性問題にまったく関心のない人が一定数います．#MeToo 運動は決してプロフェミニスト男性やフェミニスト女性のためだけに展開された運動ではありません．#MeToo 運動

2　最初のフェミニズムは「第一波フェミニズム」と呼ばれ，女性参政権を求める宣言が出され，財産権や教育の平等も達成目標として掲げられました．第二波フェミニズムでは意識高揚運動として性別役割分業の廃絶等の訴えがなされ，その後第三波フェミニズム（ポストフェミニズム）ではさらなる多様性が問題提起されることになります．

3　SNS 上で #（ハッシュタグ）を用いて意見発信をする社会運動を指します．

は，性別，人種，国籍，さらには当事者性を越えた，すべての人に開かれたデジ
タル時代を代表するフェミニズム運動なのです．それでは，読者のみなさん，共
に男性視点からとらえ直すフェミニズム研究の旅に出発しましょう．

The #MeToo Movement and Male Feminists

TABLE OF CONTENTS

1. Introduction

Entering the twenty-first century, male privilege seemed on the wane in the United States. Many took pains to avoid emphasizing traditional masculinity and power in public. Some men in media behaved in ways that just a decade earlier might have been considered "soft" or even "effeminate" with their displays of more tender and caring traits. Such trends, however, do not mean conventional performative masculinity has been eliminated. Despite the movement toward gender equality in the United States, many examples of misogyny yet remain, including specifically horrific acts of sexual harassment and sexual assault, including rape. This chapter examines the current American #MeToo movement. As a male gender scholar, I will show that men too can learn to understand women's issues and become feminists or at the very least allies of feminism. Designating male sexual assault in Hollywood as a starting point, the following pages discuss how a male perspective on such women's issues can be significant and insightful in bringing gender integration.

2. Feminism/Gender Studies and Positionality

Because the study of feminism birthed the field of gender studies, the majority of its active scholars are women. Needless to say, most #MeToo movement participants are women. Actor Emma Watson, famous for her role as Hermione in the *Harry Potter* films, defines feminism in her 2014 United Nations speech as "the belief that men and women should have equal rights and opportunities.

It is the theory of the political, economic and social equality of the sexes."[4] Here, she uses the term "sexes," however, the central goal of feminism is to deny that biological sex determines one's sexual identity. Instead of using the term sex, feminism emphasizes the use of the term gender to describe one's at-times-fluid sexual identity. The phrase "gender is learned, it is a social construct" has become almost a cliché for feminist scholars such as Judith Butler. Accordingly, sex organs are not the best way to identify gender and sexuality. Instead behaviors and preferences must be considered to understand fully a person's gender identity. The field of gender studies owes a massive debt to the female scholars who pioneered the field while simultaneously fighting for equal rights in the public sphere.[5]

No one doubts women make up the main participants of the feminist movement. But does feminism exist only for women? What about the differences between women? Watson's speech only opens the door to define feminism, leaving out ones dealing with race, ethnicity, age, sexuality, religion, nationality, and so forth. Some black feminists have argued what we know as feminism is mainly created and defined by white women and so does not necessarily apply fully to black women's lives.[6] In contrast, some gay and profeminist men appreciate the "second wave" feminism of the 1960s (the "first wave" was the late-nineteenth and early twentieth-century struggles to achieve women's voting rights) for giving them a way to further sexual liberation. These examples alone indicate that feminism is not a monolithic block of solidarity among women.

Although some profeminist men sympathize with the American #MeToo movement over Twitter, the vast majority of tweets come from women, especially semi-biographical stories about pain and suffering. The idea of gender positionality — that only women can describe the problems and come up with solutions to situations hurting women — is an early and important idea in

---

4   Emma Watson, "Emma Watson: Gender equality is your issue too," *UN Women* online, September 20, 2014, https://www.unwomen.org/en/news/stories/2014/9/emma-watson-gender-equality-is-your-issue-too.

5   Judith Butler, *Gender Trouble: Feminism and the Subversion of Identity* (New York: Routledge, 1990), 9.

6   Black feminists, such as bell hooks see men not as their enemies, but allies. See bell hooks, *Feminism Is for Everybody: Passionate Politics* (Cambridge, MA: South End Press, 2000).

the creation of gender studies. Similarly, some male profeminists search for ways to make gender visible to the eyes of men by writing about themselves.[7] Importantly, this conceptual framework is not disrespecting feminism, but instead shows how important men's engagement with feminism is. Without a doubt, the #MeToo movement benefits from male participation, as profeminist men work to de-masculinize in order to "be themselves." Since the emergence of men's liberation movement in 1970s America, profeminist men have slowly learned to release themselves from traditional male gender roles and live comfortably. In sum, by discussing both female and male experiences, feminism has brought knowledge to all seeking sustained social change, including the male ability to seek self-liberation.

3. The #MeToo Movement and Hollywood

On October 5, 2017, the *New York Times* published an article by Jodi Kantor and Megan Twohey about Hollywood film producer Harvey Weinstein's decades of widespread sexual abuse, causing quick condemnation of the powerful man amongst the public and within the film industry. On October 15, 2017, female television actor Alyssa Milano, taking a friend's suggestion, decided to use her Twitter account in an attempt to expose what heretofore had been kept in the dark: the enormous number of women subjected to unwanted

Figure 1   Alyssa Milano, Twitter post, October 2017, 1:21 p.m.
[https://twitter.com/Alyssa_Milano]

---

7   Michael Kimmel, *Manhood in America: A Cultural History* (New York: The Free Press, 1996), 1-3.

sexual advances and even sexual assault.

Milano's first "me too" tweet instantly caught the attention of broader female audiences, and quickly thousands of women started retweeting to share their own personal stories. This was the beginning of what we know today as the #MeToo movement. By the way, Milano had used the phrase "me too" without knowing a female black anti-rape activist named Tarana Burke first used the phrase "me too" on her Myspace page back in 2006.[8]

#MeToo was not the first time a social movement sought to work toward gender equality by exposing bad behavior. Besides Burke's activism, a British feminist writer named Laura Bates started a project called Everyday Sexism in 2012. It was an attempt by women to make global sexism more visible. Across the Atlantic Ocean only five years later, *New York Times* journalists Kantor and Twohey began the American version of the Everyday Sexism Project with their Weinstein article. While Weinstein was the first to fall, like a chain reaction further credible accusations of sexual abuse perpetrated by male celebrities such as Roman Polanski, Woody Allen, and Bill Cosby became public one after another. Comedian and former television star Cosby even served jail time for rape.

What is important to be noted here is that what started in Hollywood grew to include further sustainable feminist activism, such as #TimesUp, an effort to stop sexual harassment and abuse. Hollywood had long been a male-dominated homosocial world, with lurid rumors of the "casting couch" prevalent for decades if not the entire century of the film industry's existence.[9] Obviously, the #MeToo movement's main emphasis at its early stage was to reveal male sexual harassment and sexual assault in this gigantic male-centered industry. Often during accusations of sexual assault, lawyers involved in the normally private and secret settlements did so due to fear of the difficulty in proving allegations in criminal or civil court, as well as to prioritize remuneration. As a consequence, female voices too often went unnoticed and unheard. The public never knew how wide-spread sexual misconduct was until the #MeToo movement broke the story wide open. Taking place on the pub-

---

8   Carly Gieseler, *The Voices of #MeToo: From Grassroots Activism to a Viral Roar* (Lanham, Maryland: Rowman & Littlefield, 2019), 2.

9   The "homosocial" is a concept to describe non-sexual relationships between members of the same sex, often perceived as strong male bonding based on power games. The term was first coined by a feminist scholar Eve K. Sedgwick.

lic internet far outside the courtroom, the #MeToo movement successfully revealed the unheard female voices of not only those in the United States but those all over the world.

While the feminist #MeToo movement started with an exposé of sexual assault in Hollywood, it should not be forgotten that the film industry has also long been exploiting some male actors with the casting couch, albeit far less often. In the golden age of Hollywood during the 1950s, some actors such as James Dean were forced to engage in homosexual activity with gay producers to land roles.[10] Other than Dean, few confessions about sexual harassment in relation to homosexual activity have made by actors. Two brave exceptions are Cory Feldman and Brendan Fraser. Feldman, who got his start as a child actor in *The Goonies* (1985), disclosed his experience of being sexually abused in the entertainment business as a minor. Fraser, a leading man in many blockbuster films of the 2000s, made his own #MeToo statement, explaining he had endured a sexual assault in at the hands of a powerful journalist.[11]

In sum, male-centered Hollywood industry targeted not only women, but men in its insatiable sexual exploitation. In a shopping center across the street from the famous TCL Chinese Theater on Hollywood Boulevard, where movies have premiered since 1927, there is a photogenic spot for tourists to take a picture with the ironic sculpture of larger-than-life casting couch (due to be removed by the summer of 2022 after an outcry that started just after the start of the #MeToo movement).[12] How many tourists took pictures or selfies in front of giant fiberglass couch without thinking of the many lives damaged or ruined by sexual harassment and assault?

10　See Joe Hyams and Jay Hyams, *James Dean: Little Boy Lost* (London: Arrow Books, 1994).

11　*My Truth: The Rape of 2 Coreys*, directed by Brian Herzlinger (Truth 4222 Productions, 2020); and Kirsten Chuba, "Brendan Fraser Says HFPA Ex-President Sexually Assaulted Him," *Variety*, Feb 22, 2018, https://variety.com/2018/film/news/brendan-fraser-hfpa-ex-president-sexually-assaulted-him-1202707850/

12　Shane Reiner-Roth, "Controversial sculptures at Hollywood & Highland removed during $100 million mall makeover," *Architect's Newspaper*, August 5, 2021 https://www.archpaper.com/2021/08/controversial-sculptures-hollywood-highland-removed-during-100-million-makeover/

4. Male Voices

In the second U.S. presidential debate of 2016, host Anderson Cooper challenged candidate Donald J. Trump over leaked recordings made from discarded edits of a 2005 *Access Hollywood* television show interview. Trump's response led to a contentious debate about gender.

Anderson: You called what you said locker room banter. You described kissing women without consent, grabbing their genitals. That is sexual assault. You bragged that you have sexually assaulted women. Do you understand that?
Trump: This was locker room talk. I'm not proud of it. I apologize to my family. I apologize to the American people. Certainly I'm not proud of it but this is locker room talk.

"Locker room talk" is vernacular for homosocial men in male-only settings telling each other off-color stories and jokes about women. Ironically, Trump's response here explicitly illustrates that true toxic masculinity can be heard from such a closed space far more often than in public. The fact that he still won the presidential election after being revealed as a crass sexual predator proved there still is room for such an archetypal misogynistic man within the United States.

There are unintended consequences for the #MeToo movement, however. It faces backlash, division, and negative attitudes from some men, as the 2018 *Bloomberg* article "Wall Street Rule for the #MeToo Era: Avoid Women at All Cost" explains.[13] Well-established Wall Street men, who might be tempted to use their power to take advantage of women, stayed indifferent or even hostile to the feminist movement in the same way as did Trump. *Harvard Business Review* article "The #MeToo Backlash" (2019) investigates both female and male attitudes toward employment and gender after #MeToo. A survey in the article conducted at the height of #MeToo (from 2018 to 2019) shows male attitudes toward women in a business setting turned even more negative. For example, 16% of men said that they would be more reluctant to hire

---

13   Gillian Tan and Katia Porzecanski, "Wall Street Rule for the #MeToo Era: Avoid Women at All Cost," *Bloomberg*, December 3, 2018, https://www.bloombergquint.com/markets/a-wall-street-rule-for-the-metoo-era-avoid-women-at-all-cost.

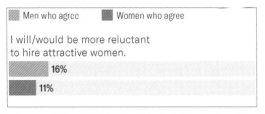

Figure 2　Source: "The #MeToo Backlash," September-October 2019

attractive women in 2018, whereas the percentage rose to 19% in a 2019 follow-up survey. Other survey questions saw similar growth in anti-women feelings. As also suggested in *Bloomberg* article's title, this type of survey data clearly indicates that men have become more careful and self-defensive toward associating with women after #MeToo.[14] One must note that these voices undoubtedly come from men clinging to male chauvinism; they perhaps enjoy dirty jokes about women the same way what Trump did with his locker room talk, fear being unable to continue their harassment, or worry about being falsely accused (an event that actually rarely happens with sexual harassment or assault charges).

Not all corporate leaders feel animosity toward the #MeToo movement. Business executive Richard Stimac writes, "The #MeToo movement is about basic human rights."[15] Other men (not necessarily profeminist) willingly spoke out in support of the movement in various ways. With #IHave on social medias, some men straightforwardly took responsibility for their past sexist actions, similar to 1970s reflective journal writings in men's encounter groups—the first organized attempt to push away from toxic masculinity by talking about their feelings and emotions, plus a way to obtain some measure of work/life balance. One male #IHave reflection written on Medium, an American online publishing platform, confesses:

> I have committed sexual assault. In junior high, my friends and I would
> go to concerts and grab women's butts in the crowds. We would compare

14　"The #MeToo Backlash," *Harvard Business Review*, September-October 2019, https://hbr.org/2019/09/the-metoo-backlash.

15　Richard Stimac, "A Role for Men in the #MeToo Movement," *American Society of Association Executives*, August 20, 2018, https://www.asaecenter.org/en/resources/articles/an_plus/2018/august/a-role-for-men-in-the-metoo-movement.

numbers...Also in high school, at a party, I held a male classmate from behind to make him think a woman he might be interested in was making a move on him, trying to dance with him. He turned around and got upset.[16]

Most of #IHave posts over social medias are either a confession of sin or reflection over poor behavior. The #HowIWillChange goes even further, as the only way to end sexual harassment and assault is to change male behavior. This new hashtag movement seeks to remake culture by educating young men and boys to treat women as equals and to call out misogyny whenever it appears.[17] Of course, the majority of men have remained silent and have not posted examples of their past transgressions or engaged in efforts to stop the current rape culture.

Besides those men apologizing for past behavior or working to prevent sexual assault, some men responded to the #MeToo movement as sexual assault survivors. "I'm a male and also a victim of a predators. Predators exist everywhere. Equally," says one male respondent.[18] As Carly Gieseler, author of *The Voices of #MeToo* and professor of performing arts, explains, there are many positive and insightful messages within #MeToo spaces:

The #MeToo movement offers a message to boys and young men that the falling icons of wealth and fame are not merely impotent role models — they are inept as human beings. Yet the movement also stresses that there are boys and men who are superior role models and remarkable human beings.[19]

Gieseler also encourages both men and women not to become "bystanders," but instead "upstanders" willing to challenge "the perpetrator/man victim/

---

16 Pierce Delahunt, "#IHave," *Medium*, December 17, 2017, https://medium.com/delapierced/ihave-e101242a8991.

17 M. E. PettyJohn, F. K. Muzzey, M. K. Maas, and H. L. McCauley, "#HowIWillChange: Engaging Men and Boys in the #MeToo Movement," *Psychology of Men & Masculinities* 20 (Oct. 2019): 612–22.

18 Gieseler, *Voices of #MeToo*, 155.

19 *Ibid.*, 161.

woman binary."[20] Instead of refusing to get involved, the upstanders speak out when breaches of decorum occur. Just like how Richard Nixon described people who do not express their opinions in public as the "silent majority" in a 1969 speech, the evasive sexists are bystanders who avoid expressing their objection to discrimination in public, although they are fully aware of its injustice. Yet even though the #MeToo movement is an iconic movement of the digital age, too often advocacy on social media has become an echo chamber that has little chance to spread its message to the uninformed.[21]

While there is likely no way to change the habits of misogynists like Trump who enjoy demeaning women in private, the larger category of evasive sexists are open to change. Therefore, what is more important here is not to criticize them by creating new terms such as "mansplaining,"[22] but rather correct the misperception of feminism being anti-male activism or stigmatizing profeminist men as either effeminate or gay. Welcoming active male participation in this feminism movement, rather than persistently criticizing men, is key to further change in American society. To contradict John Gray's famous book title *Men Are from Mars, Women Are from Venus* (1992), men and women are humans from the same planet need to treat each other equally.

5. Conclusion

Regardless of gender-free atmosphere created by some of those mentioned above, the #MeToo movement is usually recognized as a female experience, performed for women, and too often judged negatively or simply ignored by men. To respond to the social change brought by the movement, the tendency of revising some terms and expressions peculiar to the feminine and the masculine within the mainstream society have accelerated, with compliance in mind — "Ladies and gentleman," "boys and girls," and "hey guys" are phrases considered to mean "everyone," even though many people are refusing to be pigeon-holed into the male/female binary. In writing, instead of starting a

---

20　*Ibid.*, 162.
21　Echo chamber refers to the closed space of social media, where the users tend to only share the common thoughts and opinions.
22　"Mansplaining" is a portmanteau of the two words "man" and "explain." It literally means that men look down on women, explaining something simple in a patronizing way as if they would have little knowledge about the issue. See Rebecca Solnit, *Men Explain Things to Me* (Chicago: Haymarket Books, 2014).

letter with "Dear Sirs" or "Dear Sir or Madam," the use of the person's actual name or position is strongly recommended today. Besides de-gendering position titles like firefighter instead of fireman or chair instead of chairman to avoid unconscious discrimination toward women, American culture has begun to make considerations for transgender and non-binary people, such as "all-gender toilets," the use of preferred name and pronoun, and the freedom to wear colors and clothes regardless of gender assigned at birth.

Although great strides have been made, including through the #MeToo movement, misogyny remains most likely because in most of the world, human society has always been male-centered and male-dominated. To enact change, what is important is for men to face feminism and seek to treat women equally, even though there are cultural challenges. "I openly embrace the label of bad feminist. I do so because I am flawed and human. I am not terribly well versed in feminist history," writes English professor Roxane Gay, seeking to encourage people to become feminists.[23] For example, she expresses how much she loves the color of pink and enjoys groovy misogynistic music composed by men, but she can still be a feminist and considers herself such. This scholarly positionality gives opportunities for feminist men as well. It is fine for men to enjoy musicals or romance films, for example. So evasive sexists are those who can be swayed to the side of the feminists because of they can be shown injustice and discrimination faced by women, unlike those male chauvinists that reject female concerns out of hand. Evasive sexists lack courage at the moment to enact change, but with effort can be brought around toward equality.

From Seattle WTO protests in 1999 to Occupy Wall Street and Black Lives Matter in 2010s, social movements including #MeToo in the past few decades used social media to spread their message and organize for change. The diversification of the internet has created a stir in discrimination issues, enabling the individual voices to take on entrenched political power. Before these changes, gender issues were mainly addressed to only a small audience, intellectuals in academia. The participation of non-intellectual amateurs in #MeToo movement raises the further possibility of opening the door of feminism. After all, as bell hooks titled one of her many books, "feminism is for everybody."

---

23 Roxane Gay, *Bad Feminist: Essays* (New York: Harper Perennial, 2014), x.

References

Benshoff, Harry M, and Sean Griffin. *America on Film: Representing Race, Class, Gender, and Sexuality at the Movies*. Malden, MA: Wiley-Blackwell, 2009.

Brooks, Ben, and Quinton Winter. *Stories for Boys Who Dare to Be Different: True Tales of Amazing Boys Who Changed the World without Killing Dragons*. London: Quercus, 2018.

Butler, Judith. *Gender Trouble: Feminism and the Subversion of Identity*. New York: Routledge, 1990.

Connell, Robert W. *Masculinities*. Cambridge, UK: Polity Press, 2005.

Gray, John. *Men Are from Mars, Women Are from Venus: a Practical Guide for Improving Communication and Getting What You Want in Your Relationships*. New York: HarperCollins, 1992. hooks, bell. *Feminism Is for Everybody: Passionate Politics*. Cambridge, MA: South End Press, 2000.

Hyams, Joe, and Jay Hyams. *James Dean: Little Boy Lost*. London: Arrow Books, 1994.

Kantor, Jodi, and Megan Twohey. *She Said: Breaking the Sexual Harassment Story That Helped Ignite a Movement*. New York: Penguin Press, 2019.

Kimmel, Michael. *Manhood in America: A Cultural History*. New York: The Free Press, 1996.

PettyJohn, M. E., F. K. Muzzey, M. K. Maas, and H. L. McCauley. "#HowIWillChange: Engaging Men and Boys in the #MeToo Movement." *Psychology of Men & Masculinities* 20 (Oct. 2019): 612–22.

Reiner-Roth, Shane. "Controversial sculptures at Hollywood & Highland removed during $100 million mall makeover." *Architect's Newspaper*, August 5, 2021. https://www.archpaper.com/2021/08/controversial-sculptures-hollywood-highland-removed-during-100-million-makeover/

Sedgwick, Eve K. *Between Men: English Literature and Male Homosocial Desire*. New York: Columbia University Press, 1985.

Solnit, Rebecca. *Men Explain Things to Me*. Chicago: Haymarket Books, 2014.

Stimac, Richard. "A Role for Men in the #MeToo Movement." *American Society of Association Executives*, August 20, 2018. https://www.asaecenter.org/en/resources/articles/an_plus/2018/august/a-role-for-men-in-the-metoo-movement.

Tan, Gillian, and Katia Porzecanski. "Wall Street Rule for the #MeToo Era:

Avoid Women at All Cost." *Bloomberg* online, December 3, 2018. https://
www.bloombergquint.com/markets/a-wall-street-rule-for-the-metoo-era-
avoid-women-at-all-cost.

| Further Reading

Gay, Roxane. *Bad Feminist: Essays*. New York: Harper Perennial, 2014.
Gieseler, Carly. *The Voices of #MeToo: From Grassroots Activism to a Viral Roar*. Lanham, Maryland: Rowman & Littlefield, 2019.

| 日本語文献案内

上野千鶴子『女ぎらい：ニッポンのミソジニー』朝日文庫，2018 年.
チママンダ・ンゴズィ・アディーチェ『男も女もみんなフェミニストでなきゃ』
　河出書房新社，2017 年.
水島新太郎『マンガでわかる男性学：ジェンダーレス時代を生きるために』改訂
　版，行路社，2018 年.

| 考えてみよう

1. アメリカで始まった #MeToo 運動は，女性だけでなく一部のプロフェミニ
　スト男性たち，さらには世界中の人々が参加したフェミニズム運動です．人
　種差別や格差問題など，世界ではさまざまな問題を抱える人たちがいます．
　国境や当事者性を超えてこれらの問題を考える意義について今一度考えてみ
　ましょう．非当事者が社会運動に参加することで，もたらされる変化につい
　て具体例をあげてみましょう．

2. 2021 年 3 月，世界の男女格差を数値化するジェンダーギャップ指標が発表
　されました．日本の総合スコアは 0.656 で，調査対象である 156 か国中
　120 位と，ジェンダー平等社会というにはほど遠い順位でした．2006 年か
　ら続けられていた東京医科大学による女性受験者の点数操作，男性誌「週刊
　SPA!」による女子大学の性的ランク付け問題（2018 年 12 月 25 日号），
　東京オリンピック組織委員会会長森喜朗による女性蔑視発言（2021 年 2 月
　3 日）など，日本にはなぜ女性蔑視な社会通念が依然として根づいているの
　でしょうか．身近な問題を例に考えてみましょう．

・・・・・・・・・・・・・・・・・・・・・・・・・・・・・・・・・・・・・

水島　新太郎
Shintaro MIZUSHIMA

太平洋世界における人の移動

Japanese Women of the Fishing Industry in Hawai'i

概要

　この章では，アメリカ研究（American Studies）の立場から，ハワイ，移民，女性をキーワードとして，太平洋世界における人の移動について考察します．アメリカ研究は歴史，文学，民族誌などを含む分野横断的な側面をもっています．本章は主に文献資料を使用する歴史学的な手法を用いた研究を取り上げますが，とりわけ研究対象が女性や労働者階級，いわゆる庶民の場合は文書記録が残らないことも多いため，直接関係者に会って聞き取り調査や資料収集を伴うフィールドワークも積極的に行います．

　また本章には海を生活の拠りどころとする漁民や漁村が頻繁に登場します．これは陸中心的な視点である landscape に代わって seascape，つまり海に視点を移すことによって，陸からでは決して見えてこない新たな景色があることを紹介するためです．

図1　ホノルルの造船所にて日本式サンパン漁船，紀南丸の進水式．左から2人目が大谷松治郎，4人目が船主の清水松太郎，右端が清水ハル．このとき，清水家の静枝は日本に足止めされており，写真に写っていない［テルオ船井所蔵］

国際英語文化と太平洋世界研究

　人類（ホモ・サピエンス）の歴史は移動の歴史でもあります．30 〜 10 万年前にアフリカ大陸に出現した人類は，その後，世界中に拡散しました．人類が日本列島にやってきたのは今から 3 万年以上前のことで，日本人の祖先は大陸から歩いてやってくるルートに加えて，当時大陸とつながっていた台湾から，世界最大級の海流である黒潮を船で越えて琉球列島にやってきたと考えられています．また人類のアメリカ大陸への拡散も，氷河期に陸続きとなっていたベーリング海峡を徒歩で渡っただけでなく，太平洋の島々から船で大陸に到達したことが近年の研究で明らかになってきました．

　さて，それでは国際英語文化と本章のテーマである太平洋の研究は，どのように結びつくのでしょうか．また太平洋世界の一部である日本，アメリカ，そしてハワイの関係を，どのように理解したらよいのでしょうか．日本はよく，「四方を海で囲まれた島国」といわれ，まるで世界の潮流から隔絶された歴史をたどってきたような印象をもつ人もいます．しかし，海は人々を隔てるだけでなく，人々をつなぐ役割も果たしてきたことを忘れてはいけません．「四方を海に向かって開かれた」日本は古来，近隣地域の人々と海を介した交流を重ねてきました．いわゆる「鎖国」政策をとっていた江戸時代でも，特に漁民は魚を追いかけてあちこちに出漁し，やがて朝鮮半島沖や蝦夷地（北海道），さらに樺太にまで進出して，アイヌなど現地の人々と水産物などの交易を行っています．

　このように海を縦横無尽に動く漁民たちは，正式な日本の開国を待たずに民間レベルの国際交流を展開しました．例えば土佐の漁民である万次郎は，1841（天保 12）年，14 歳のときに仲間 4 人とともに出漁し，嵐にあって無人島に漂着した後，アメリカの捕鯨船に救出されました．万次郎らを乗せた捕鯨船が補給と休息のために向かったのがハワイです．その頃のハワイは，1810 年にカメハメハ大王がハワイ諸島を統一して打ち立てたハワイ王朝の支配下にあり，太平洋捕鯨の基地として栄えていました．そのハワイは万次郎らを温かく迎え入れます．その後，捕鯨船の船長に誘われてアメリカ本土へ渡って教育を受け，ジョン万次郎と呼ばれるようになった彼は，金鉱が発見されたカリフォルニアで金を採掘して資金を貯め，ハワイに戻って仲間と合流したのち 1851（嘉永 4）年に日本への帰国を果たします．その翌々年にペリーが来航すると，ジョン万次郎はアメリカでの経験を生かして船舶技術や航海術，英語の伝授などを通して，日本の近代化に貢献することになります．

　漂流という形ではなく，日本が初めて海外に集団移民を送り出したのは 1868（明治元）年のことで，行先はハワイでした．その後，明治政府とハワイ王国の

取り決めによって，1885（明治16）年に官約移民が開始されると，ハワイへ向かう日本人の数は増加し，日本のハワイ・真珠湾攻撃によって太平洋戦争が始まる直前には総人口の約37%を日本人移住者とその子孫が占めるまでになりました．リゾート地としてのイメージが強いハワイですが，実は観光だけでなく，ビジネスや文化，教育などさまざまな面で，今日でも日本と強い結びつきをもっています．

　また，ハワイには，日本もハワイと同じく太平洋に浮かぶ島であり仲間だとみなす感覚がありました．ハワイ王朝7代目君主であるカラカウア王は，ハワイへの経済的，政治的影響力を増大させるアメリカに対抗するため，日本を含む太平洋の島々と同盟関係を結ぼうとします．また上記のように，明治政府に働きかけて官約移民を開始したのもこの王様です．そのような願いもむなしく1898年にハワイはアメリカに併合されますが，これはハワイ王朝最後の君主であるリリウオカラニ女王をはじめとするハワイ人の意向を無視した，アメリカによる一方的な政治的決定でした．

　高校の世界史の教科書などでは，アメリカが主にイギリスなど欧州からの移民と，アフリカから奴隷として強制的に連れてこられた人々やその子孫によってつくり上げられた大西洋国家であると記述されることが多いのですが，アメリカをハワイ，そして日本といった太平洋側から描くことによって初めて見えてくる特徴があります．そもそもなぜ，幕末にアメリカの捕鯨船が日本近海までやって来るようになったのでしょうか．どうしてアメリカはハワイ人の反対を押し切ってハワイを併合したのでしょうか．さらに明治以降，多くの日本人がハワイをめざしたのはなぜなのでしょうか．アメリカもハワイも日本も，ともに太平洋世界を形成する重要な構成員です．それらの関係性をひも解くためのこのような問いは，国際英語圏文化における太平洋世界の研究の重要性を示唆しています．

研究の楽しさ

　私は大学時代，日本史を学んでいました．卒業論文で第二次世界大戦直後のGHQ（連合国軍最高司令官総司令部）による「女性解放」政策を取り上げたことをきっかけに，日米関係についてもっと知りたいと思うようになりました．しかし国際関係や外交史の研究で注目されるのはエリート男性ばかりで，女性や民族的マイノリティ（少数派）などは出る幕すらありません．長い間，公の舞台から除外されていたためです．

　しかし民間レベルの国際交流に目を向けると，前述のジョン万次郎のような人物に加えて女性たちの存在も浮かび上がってきます．例えば欧米の女性は長年，

キリスト教を基盤とする国際的ネットワークを築き上げ，社会福祉活動や反戦平和運動などに従事してきました．そして明治以降は日本人女性も，そのような運動に積極的に関わります．さらにアメリカでは，戦前，日本人移民は参政権を与えられず，政治の場から排除されていたのですが，ハワイへ渡った日本人漁民は，持ち前の高い漁労技術や海に関する豊富な知識を生かして，ハワイの支配層である白人政財界指導者たちと一緒に水産業の新興をはかります．政治力をもたないはずの日本人漁民（男女とも）が現地の水産業を支え，政策に大きな影響を与えていたのは興味深い現象です．

　女性や民族マイノリティの視点に立って世界をとらえ直すと，新しい世界が見えてきます．その色彩豊かな景色に，私はいつもワクワクさせられています．

この章のトピック

　ハワイには現在，マジョリティ（多数派）の民族が存在せず，日系人をはじめとするアジア系，白人，ハワイ人などさまざまな民族的背景をもつ人々が暮らしています．本章の英語本文は，特に女性，そして民族マイノリティという2つの要素をもつハワイの日本人女性移民の体験を扱っています．ハワイでは戦前，砂糖きびプランテーションを所有する白人が現地の政治経済を支配していました．ハワイへ渡った日本人の多くはプランテーションで働きましたが，そこで女性は従属的な地位に立たされていた上に，家父長制度によって家庭でも抑圧される存在とみなされてきました．家長の判断でハワイ在住の見知らぬ男性と写真を交換し，「写真花嫁」としてハワイに嫁いで愛のない苦しい人生を送ったというのが，日本人女性移民に対する定説でした．しかしそのような家父長制度は，長男が単独で土地を相続する農村経済に起因するもので，土地をもたず，個人の技量によって生業を営む漁村には当てはまりません．陸（農村）から海（漁村）へと私たちの視点を変換することによって，抑圧された写真花嫁のイメージとは異なる，生き生きとした漁村女性たちの日常が見えてくるはずです．

研究の素材

　研究にとって欠かせないのは一次史（資）料，つまり当時の人々が残した記録を入手することです．公文書と呼ばれる政府の記録や，企業や団体などの文書，さらに個人が残すメモや日記，写真や手紙，当時の新聞や雑誌の記事といったさまざまな記録を使います．そのため図書館や資料館だけでなく，関係者の個人宅や

お寺, 神社, 教会などを訪問することもあります. また研究対象となる場所を訪ねて, その「空気」を肌で感じることも大切です.

　文書記録の収集に加えて, 関係者への聞き取り調査を行うこともあります. その際に留意すべきなのは, 過去の記憶は美化されたり, 編集, つまり都合よく切り貼りされたりするということです. もっとも, そのような情報の偏りや記憶・記録の改変は, すべての一次史(資)料に存在します. 新聞や雑誌の記事は記者というフィルターを通して書かれます. また一見「中立公平」に見える公文書も, 誰が何を記録し, 何を記録しないか, 何のために記録するか, といったさまざまな判断を経て作成されます.

　そのため, 集めた一次史(資)料の特質を見きわめた上で分析する過程が欠かせません. いわゆる史料批判という作業です. そのでき具合が研究の質に直結します.

研究がめざすこと

　ある研究テーマについて, 多分こうだろうという仮説をたて, 関連する一次史(資)料を集めて精査していくうちに, 仮説が根底から崩れてしまうことがあります. 期待していた情報が何も手に入らなかったり, 逆に予測をはるかに上回る新たな事実がわかったりするからです. もっとも, 大きな金脈を掘り当てるような大発見はきわめて稀で, 研究のほとんどは, 小さな砂粒を一粒一粒丁寧に積み上げて富士山をつくり上げていくような, 地味で根気のいる作業の連続です. それでも, これまで世界中の誰も知らなかった新たな事(史)実を明らかにする喜びは何物にも代え難いです. 放っておけば歴史の闇の中に永遠に埋もれてしまったかもしれない出来事を発掘して後世に残すこと, それが研究の目的であり, 価値でもあるのです.

Japanese Women of the Fishing Industry in Hawai'i

TABLE OF CONTENTS

5. Conclusion: The Legacy of Japanese Fishing Culture in Hawai'i

1. Introduction

What kind of image do you have about Hawai'i? The tropical Waikiki Beach or the elegant hula? Many people think of Hawai'i as a great beach resort attraction, but only a few people know that Hawai'i used to be an independent kingdom. The Hawaiian Kingdom was established by King Kamehameha the Great in 1810, but it was overthrown by a coup d'état, which led to the establishment of a republic in 1893; in 1898, the Republic of Hawai'i was annexed by the United States, becoming an American territory. Hawai'i became the fiftieth US state in 1959.

Today, the population of Hawai'i has much more racial diversity than the United States as a whole, because it has received many immigrants from various countries in Asia, the Pacific region, and Europe as well as from the continental US. One of the most prominent ethnic groups in Hawai'i has been people of Japanese ancestry, or Japanese Americans. Since the Hawaiian Kingdom reached an agreement with the Meiji government in 1885 to accept government contract labor immigrants, or *kan'yaku imin*, many Japanese have immigrated to Hawai'i. In the early 1940s, about 37% of population in Hawai'i was Japanese, along with their *nisei* children with American citizenship.[1]

This essay examines the history of Japanese immigrants in Hawai'i, in particular, the women of Japanese fishing communities. Although most Japanese immigrants worked in the sugarcane industry, which dominated the Hawaiian economy before the Pacific War, some engaged in fishing operations instead. By the late 1920s, Japanese fisherfolk[2] established modern commercial fisheries, in which both men and women played important roles. When looking at the literature of Japanese women, a defining image stands out: a poor

---

1 In the United States, children born on its soil obtain US citizenship (*jus soli*, or right of the soil), while children born to parents who are Japanese nationals also obtain Japanese nationality (*jus sanguinis*, or right of blood). Therefore, *nisei* children of Japanese immigrants in Hawai'i and other places in the United States often had double citizenship.

2 In Hawai'i, fishing was predominantly a male business, but some women also engaged in fishing operations. Therefore, this essay often uses "fisherfolk" as a gender-neutral term.

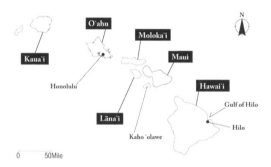

Figure 1   Hawaiian Islands

"picture bride" who was forcibly shipped off to a strange land to marry a strange man after exchanging pictures, leading to a hard life.[3] In contrast to such a well-known image of these women as passive victims of patriarchal oppression, this essay reveals the realities of the diverse and dynamic practices of Japanese women in Hawai'i.

2.   The Development of Japanese Fisheries in Hawai'i and the Formation of Fishing Communities

Most Japanese immigrants during the early days were single men, but there were women, too, and some of them engaged in fishing and peddling. Nobu Kurihara of the island of Kasasa off the coast of Suō-Ōshima in Yamaguchi prefecture came to Hawai'i in 1885 on the *City of Tokio* as one of the first government contract laborers with her husband and children. After working at a sugar mill on the island of Hawai'i, Nobu moved to the island of O'ahu with her family and started fishing and farming.[4] Jinkurō Ōhara's wife contributed to her family finances by peddling fish. After Jinkurō, originally from Agenoshō of Suō-Ōshima sailed out and filled his boat with fish, his wife sold the catch on plantations on the island of Kaua'i and made dozens of dollars in profit.[5]

---

3   See *Picture Bride*, directed by Kayo Hatta (1995; Miramax).
4   Nippu Jijisha, *Kan'yaku Imin Hawai tokō goju-shūnen kinenshi* (Honolulu: Nippu Jijisha, 1935), 19.
5   Wakayamaken, ed., *Wakayamaken iminshi* (Wakayama: Wakayama prefectural government, 1957), 511.

These accounts suggest that early Japanese settlers brought gender[6] roles distinctive of the coastal areas from their home villages to Hawai'i. In Suō-Ōshima, women called *katagi* peddled fish throughout the island. The highly gendered role of fish peddling had been shaped to make clear profits by women directly handling hauls made by their husbands. In Hawai'i, men and women from fishing communities brought such customs from home and thus complemented each other from the early stage of commercial fishing there.

With the rapidly increasing population of Japanese in Hawai'i, the local fisheries drastically expanded because many Japanese chose fish as a primary protein source.[7] In shallow waters, native Hawaiian, Chinese, and Japanese fisherfolk engaged in fishing, while offshore fishing was completely dominated by native Hawaiians. Although they were latecomers to Hawaiian waters, the Japanese quickly adapted themselves to the natural conditions in Hawai'i and overwhelmed their rivals by introducing efficient Japanese-style fishing craft called *sampan*, gear, and skills, as well as adopting techniques that they learned from native Hawaiians. Together with Japanese community leaders, they established fishing companies around 1910, which functioned as hubs for fish distribution. In 1922, the Japanese fisheries added the Hawaiian Tuna Packers to their business circle and expanded skipjack tuna fishing by paving the way for its sale beyond the islands' markets.

The strengthened presence of Japanese in Hawaiian waters accompanied the formation of the fishing communities. Akira Ōtani was born in 1921 as the second son of fish peddler Matsujirō Ōtani from Okikamuro, an island off the coast of Suō-Ōshima in Yamaguchi prefecture. Akira grew up in Kaka'ako in Honolulu, where many fishermen and their families resided. In his childhood memories, residents of the community always helped each other and lived in a close network of families and local residents.[8] When a *sampan* came back to the Kewalo Basin, right next to the Kaka'ako district, children swarmed around it shouting "*okazu* (dish)" and obtained a free share of the catch.

6　Gender is a category of analysis to understand socially and culturally constructed differences of men and women.

7　In 1900, the number of Japanese in Hawai'i reached fifty thousand, making up nearly forty percent of the total population, and this number continued to grow. Hawai Nihonjin Iminshi Kankō Iinkai, ed. *Hawai Nihonjin Iminshi* (Honolulu: United Japanese Society of Hawaii, 1962), 311-3.

8　Interview with Akira Ōtani, Honolulu, March 3, 2008.

Figure 2　Island of Oʻahu

"Fishermen were generous," Teruo Funai recalled. Teruo was born in 1926 and grew up in Kakaʻako. He also remembered that his father, Seiichi, a boat carpenter from Wakayama prefecture, never took fish for free. Through everyday contact with fishermen, he sensed how tough their jobs were and hesitated to take advantage of their goodwill.[9]

3.　Women's Contribution to the Fishing Industry and Community Life

Matsutarō Shimizu came to Hawaiʻi in 1921 from Tanabe in Wakayama prefecture at the request of Isematsu Takenaka, a skipjack tuna fisherman originally from Tanabe. Takenaka's wife, Haru, came to Honolulu from Haya in Wakayama prefecture to join her husband in 1920 and gave birth to a daughter, Shizue, and two sons. The Takenaka family in Kakaʻako, however, did not last for long, because Isematsu died, leaving behind Haru, Shizue, and the two sons. Later, Haru married Matsutarō Shimizu. Shizue remembered that her stepfather Matsutarō always stayed out at sea because "he was a fisherman by nature."[10] Even when Matsutarō landed, he rarely stayed home. Instead, he went to the port and spent most of his time taking care of his fishing gear and *sampan*. The chronic absence of fathers was common in fishermen's households.

9　Interview with Teruo Funai, Honolulu, March 3, 2008.

10　Interview with Hisao and Shizue Shimizu, Honolulu, March 3, 2008.

Figure 3　Hawaiian Tuna Packers around the 1930s
[Photo courtesy, Hawai'i State Archives]

Children of fishermen rarely saw their fathers because they did not come home very often. Even when they were at home, they usually left home very early in the morning before the children woke up, so the children knew their mothers' faces, but didn't know their fathers'.[11]

Women's Contribution to Fish Processing

This pattern of family life spawned social and economic arrangements specific to the fishing community. While fishermen stayed out at sea, only a few of their wives chose to stay home and become full-time housewives; many of them went outside of the home and worked in fisheries-related industries. In Honolulu, the Hawaiian Tuna Packers hired many women from fishing communities. These women mainly engaged in splitting fish lengthwise and sorting the split fish by weight or length.

Shizue Shimizu remembers that "all of fishermen's wives in Kaka'ako went to the Tuna Packers for work. Their workload was not very hard. The workshift was from 7:30 am to 4 pm, and there was a thirty-minute lunch break."[12] Overall, her memory conveys that the canners hired Japanese women at low wages who worked long hours during the high season. However, there were weeks when only a few hours of work were available during the low season of skipjack tuna fishing. Such seasonality lowered the average pay

---

11　*Ibid.*
12　Interview with Shizue Shimizu, Honolulu, March 3, 2008.

rate.

Fluctuating work hours and low wages did not deter these women from engaging in manufacturing work. Besides additional income, women flocked to the canneries and other workplaces to find solace from the loneliness produced by the absence of their husbands and fathers. Moreover, co-workers helped each other with various aspects of everyday life. Because the Kaka'ako fishing community did not have formal childcare facilities, the community developed social networks that easily cut across households, occupations, and neighborhoods and reduced the burden of child rearing.

Raising Children

When Teruo Funai was a baby, his neighbor helped take care of him. His mother, Kimi, was busy taking care of her four siblings and at least six apprentice workers from her husband's shipyard in addition to looking after Teruo.[13] When Akira Ōtani's father Matsujirō started peddling fish, his mother, Kane, supported him by working at pineapple and tuna canneries while raising eight children. "I sincerely appreciate her for her great contribution," Matsujirō later said of Kane's long-term support and devotion to their family and his work.[14]

In addition to Kane's extraordinary hard work, the watchful eyes of a closely knit neighborhood, coupled with very light automobile traffic, further reduced the anxiety of childcare. Akira Ōtani always enjoyed playing baseball in the street with his friends without the fear of being hit by a car or dealing with crime. He ran away only when he hit a home run that probably damaged someone's home.[15]

Women's Contribution to Fish Sales

On top of their work in canneries and stabilizing community life through developing friendships and neighborhood ties, Japanese women made important contributions to the sales of fish. Even after the establishment of the modern market system, they engaged in fish peddling and actively interacted with consumers. Lucy Robello, a Portuguese American woman born in 1905

13　Interview with Teruo Funai, Honolulu, March 3, 2008.

14　Matsujirō Ōtani, *Waga hito to narishi ashiato: hachijū nen no kaiko* (Honolulu: M. Ōtani & Co, 1971), 34.

15　Interview with Akira Ōtani, Honolulu, March 3, 2008.

on Oʻahu, gave an interesting account of these women Japanese fish peddlers.

And anytime the fish peddlers–mostly Japanese women–would come, we had fish, because Portuguese like fish. The peddlers had the fish box in the back with chunks of ice ... When the Japanese peddlers didn't have fish, they'd come with head cabbages and sweet potatoes, and we'd buy them.[16]

This account reveals that the custom of Japanese women's fish peddling spread beyond their own ethnic enclave and reached the dinner tables of other fish-eating ethnic groups. With the peddling style they brought from Japan, they aggressively expanded this new market by selling fish door-to-door to an ethnically diverse population in Hawaiʻi, striving to meet a variety of consumer demands.

In downtown Honolulu, women's presence was important in running businesses smoothly. Matsujiro Ōtani turned his daughters, Florence and Gladys, into staff members of his seafood company, together with his sons, Jiroichi and Akira.[17] With the encouragement of his children, Matsujirō became the owner of Aʻala Market in downtown Honolulu in 1939. In the following year, a disastrous fire burned the Market, causing damage amounting to $100,000. Encouraged by his children, Ōtani undertook not only reconstruction but additions, expansions, and improvements of their facilities into the largest shopping place in Hawaiʻi in those days.

Konpira-san and kō gatherings

Wearing only a kanaka (native Hawaiian) shirt, the wife of a fisherman easily goes anywhere ... She does not mind eating only rice gruel with a tea flavor for five to ten days. Her earnest concern about the safety of her husband is, however, uncompromisingly strong. Buddhist temples and Shinto shrines receive donations from quite a few fishermen's wives.

---

16 Michi Kodama-Nishimoto, Warren S. Nishimoto, and Cynthia A. Oshiro, eds. *Hanahana: An Oral History Anthology of Hawaii's Working People* (Honolulu: Ethnic Studies Oral History Project, University of Hawaiʻi at Manoa, 1984), 80, 81.

17 "Ōtani Matsujirō-den," *Nippu Jiji* (December 4, 1941): 6.

They also willingly make generous relief donations.[18]

This portrayal of a fisherman's wife appeared in a Japanese newspaper in 1910. Beyond the frugal disposition, it emphasizes the ardent piety of fishermen's wives. The dangers of fishing and navigation inherent in their husbands' occupation compelled them to seek divine protection.

Hawai'i already had several religious sects of Buddhism and Christianity, which had taken root deeply in local Japanese society. But the *kami* of Kotohira Shrine, or "Konpira-*san*" located in Kagawa prefecture, was revered among fisherfolk and seafarers in Western Japan as a guardian deity of fishing and navigation, and when these fisherfolk came to Hawai'i, their beliefs and practices accompanied them on their trans-Pacific journey. Hawaii Kotohira Shrine in Honolulu, established around 1920, functioned as glue that held the fishing community together.[19]

While visiting Konpira-*san* in Hawai'i, the women of fishing communities actively promoted the *kō* gatherings and carried out religious ceremonies, including special services for drowning victims. Conducting recreational activities, such as sports meetings or *undō-kai* and bon dances, was also a part of the *kō* activities.[20]

4. Wartime Experience

Japan's Pearl Harbor attack on December 7 (Hawai'i time), 1941, crippled the Japanese fisheries, because the US government confiscated *sampan* and sent Japanese fisherfolk and business leaders, including Matsutarō Shimizu and Matsujirō Ōtani, to internment camps in Hawai'i and the continental US. On the West Coast, all the Japanese and their descendants, the number of which far exceeded 100,000, were interned. Hawai'i had a limited number of Japanese and their *nisei* children interned, but its Japanese population had to follow severe restrictions, such as prohibition from speaking Japanese in public spaces and closing Japanese language schools, Buddhist

18 "Gyofu no tsuma," *Hawai Shokumin Shinbun* (July 15, 1910): 2.
19 "History of the Shrine," Hawaii Kotohira Jinja Hawaii Dazaifu Tenmangu," accessed February 20, 2021, http://www.e-shrine.org/history.html.
20 "Honolulu Tsūshin" *Kamuro* 82 (May 1929): 9; *Kamuro* 90 (March 1931): 6; *Kamuro* 91 (August 1931): 6; "Hawai Honolulu Hachiman-kō no kōen," *Kamuro* 140 (May 1938): 4.

temples, and Shinto shrines.

Shizue Shimizu, stepdaughter of Matsutarō Shimizu, happened to be in Japan when the war broke out. She had nothing but living at her relative's place in Wakayama prefecture during the war. Her dual citizenship made her vulnerable to anti-American sentiment in Japan. Even some of her relatives treated her poorly.

> I don't know why one of my aunts, a blood relative, always treated me as if I had been her enemy and constantly bullied me in a condescending manner.[21]

The end of war in August 1945 did not end her hardships. Because local authorities said, "if you don't vote, we don't give you any ration of food," she reluctantly cast a vote in the first general election in Japan in 1947.[22] Soon, the US government striped her of her US citizenship. In 1953, she came back to Hawai'i and regained her citizenship after suing the US government with eight other *nisei* plaintiffs.[23]

5. Conclusion: The Legacy of Japanese Fishing Culture in Hawai'i

The extensive involvement of women in the economic and social activities of the fishing communities in Hawai'i has survived well into the twenty-first century despite the tremendous political turmoil and changes in the demography of commercial fishing. Although the Pacific War devastated the fishing industry and broke down community life, a post-war boom revitalized the Japanese fishing fleet due to fisherfolk coming back to Hawai'i from internment camps. Gradually, the Japanese population at sea has declined primarily because the younger generation did not follow in their parents' footsteps.

Starting in the early 1960s, hundreds of Okinawan fishermen came to Honolulu and reinforced the dwindling Japanese fishing fleets. Takeko Nakashima left Okinawa at the invitation of her fisherman husband, Hiroshi. As soon as she was settled in Honolulu in 1974, Takeko opened a fish shop and

---

21 Interview with Shizue Shimizu, Honolulu, March 4, 2008.
22 *Ibid.*, March 3, 2008.
23 Manako Ogawa, *Sea of Opportunity: The Japanese Pioneers of the Fishing Industry in Hawai'i* (Honolulu: University of Hawai'i Press, 2015), 124-126.

sold the fish that her husband caught.[24] While the rise of supermarkets since the late 1940s has deprived small retailers of their shoppers, old-style mom-and-pop shops, including Takeko's, continue to exist by attracting a certain number of loyal customers.

Many women like her still represent a core intersection of sea and community by selling fresh fish or manufacturing various marine products. They were, and still are, an indispensable part of the fishing industry in Hawai'i.

| References

Center for Oral History, University of Hawai'i at Manoa: Hawai'i United Okinawa Association. *Uchinanchu: A History of Okinawans in Hawaii*. Honolulu: Ethnic Studies Program, University of Hawai'i at Manoa, 1981.

Kodama-Nishimoto, Michi, Warren S. Nishimoto, and Cynthia A. Oshiro, eds. *Hanahana: An Oral History Anthology of Hawaii's Working People*. Honolulu: Ethnic Studies Oral History Project, University of Hawai'i at Manoa, 1984.

Ogawa, Manako. *Sea of Opportunity: The Japanese Pioneers of the Fishing Industry in Hawai'i*. Honolulu: University of Hawai'i Press, 2015.

| Further Reading

Hsu, Madeline Y. *Asian American History: A Very Short Introduction*. Oxford: Oxford University Press, 2017.

Koser, Khalid. *International Migration: A Very Short Introduction*. Oxford: Oxford University Press, 2016.

| 日本語文献案内

小川真和子『海をめぐる対話　ハワイと日本：水産業からのアプローチ』塙書房，2019年.

小川真和子『海の民のハワイ：ハワイの水産業を開拓した日本人の社会史』人文書院，2017年.

小川真和子「太平洋戦争中のハワイにおける日系人強制収容：消された過去を追って」『立命館言語文化研究』25巻1号，105-118，2013.

島田法子編著『写真花嫁・戦争花嫁のたどった道：女性移民史の発掘』明石書店，2009年.

24　Interview with Takeko Nakashima, Honolulu, October 3, 2009.

▌考えてみよう

　本章で論じたように，日本からハワイへの人の移動は，出身地における産業形態や信仰など，生業や社会活動，文化資産などの移動も伴いました．そしてそれらは時にホスト社会に合わせて変容しました．また戦時中における日系人の強制収容や公の場での日本語使用の禁止などは，戦争によって顕在化したホスト社会との軋轢，そして断絶を象徴する出来事でもあります．

　これらの事例を踏まえて，太平洋世界における国境を越えた人の移動の事例を調べてみましょう．本章が取り上げた 20 世紀初頭前後と比較して，グローバル化が格段に進んだ今日では，人の流れがさらに活発化しています．それは日本から太平洋世界各地へ，という動きだけでなく，逆に世界から日本へやってきたり，さらに複数の場所をさまざまなルートで移動するなど，その経路も複雑化しています．

　もしかしたら近い将来，留学や仕事，結婚などのために海外へ移動するのはあなた自身かもしれません．ですから，あなたが一番，住んでみたいと思う国や地域を取り上げて調べてみるとよいでしょう．

・・

小川　真和子
Manako OGAWA

海の歴史から見る英語圏文化

Pirates of the Caribbean: Their Images and Realities

概要

　英語圏の文化の中には海と関わりのあるものが少なくありません. なかでも「カリブの海賊」のイメージは, 映画や漫画を通して我々にもなじみの深いものとなっています. ではそのモデルとなった, 18 世紀初頭に北米やカリブ海で活動していた現実の海賊たちは, 一体どのような人々だったのでしょうか. 本章では英語圏の海事史研究の一例として, 歴史上の海賊の姿に光を当てます. さらに, この海賊たちのように過去に生きた人々の姿はいかにして明らかにしうるのか, 歴史研究の面白さとは何か, そして研究を通して得られるものは何なのかについても考えてみたいと思います.

図1　トラファルガー海戦時のネルソン提督の旗艦ヴィクトリー号［筆者撮影］

国際英語文化の中の海事史（マリタイム・ヒストリー）研究

　英語圏のうちで代表的な国というと，多くの人はまずイギリスやアメリカを思い浮かべるでしょう．ではその文化といえば何を連想するでしょうか．イギリスであればサッカーやラグビーなどのスポーツ，優雅なティータイムの文化，アメリカならば野球やハンバーガー，あるいはヒップホップかもしれません．しかし，日本に住む我々には連想しにくい，重要な要素が１つあります．それは海との関わりです．英語圏の社会や文化には，実は海洋との深い歴史的つながりがあるのです．

　まずイギリスを見てみましょう．そもそも世界各地に英語圏の国が誕生した背景には，イギリス，特にその一部であるイングランドが16世紀以降，海を通じて世界に進出し，植民地帝国を築いたということがあります．もちろんこのような帝国支配の過去は，現在はイギリスでも肯定的にとらえられているわけではありません．しかし，海洋を通して世界に進出したという事実は，今でもイギリス人のアイデンティティと深く結びついていると言えます．例えばイギリスで有名な歴史上の人物には，16世紀に中南米のスペイン領植民地を荒らし回り，アルマダ海戦（1588年）でも活躍したフランシス・ドレイクや，トラファルガー海戦（1805年）で仏西艦隊を破ったネルソン提督など，海にゆかりのある人物も多く含まれています．また，グリニッジの国立海事博物館をはじめとして，イギリス各地には小さなものも含めると，数多くの海事関係の博物館が存在します．

　一方，アメリカは大陸国家としての性格も強いため，海との関わりはイギリスほど顕著ではありませんが，その歴史にもやはり海の要素は存在します．ニューヨークやボストンといった誰もが知るアメリカの都市が，植民地期には海賊の基地でもありました．独立後の19世紀初頭になると，合衆国の商船隊は世界中に進出していきます．さらに1898年の米西戦争以降は，合衆国も海洋帝国の性格をもつようになっていきました．このように英語圏の国々，特にイギリスやアメリカと海との歴史的つながりという側面は，英語圏の社会や文化を理解する上では無視できないものなのです．

この章のトピック

　一口に海との歴史的つながりといってもさまざまなものがありますが，本章では，我々にもなじみ深いカリブの海賊イメージのもとになった，北米やカリブ海で活動していた海賊の歴史に焦点を当てます．現実の海賊たちも，イギリスの海

洋進出の歴史と深い関係がありました．またカリブの海賊は英語圏の映画の人気の題材でもあります．特にアメリカでは『グーニーズ』や『パイレーツ・オブ・カリビアン』など，海賊が主人公，あるいは海賊が深く関わる作品が繰り返し作られています．さらに，カリブの海賊をモチーフにした作品は，漫画『ONE PIECE』のように日本でも見られます．

　このように映画や漫画で知名度のある海賊ですが，現実の海賊がどのような人々であったのかについてはあまり知られていません．この章ではそのような歴史上の海賊，特に18世紀初頭の海賊の姿を，近年の研究成果をふまえて紹介します．海賊たちは血も涙もない犯罪者だったのでしょうか．あるいは映画や漫画で描かれるように勇敢なヒーローだったのでしょうか．彼ら彼女ら（女海賊もいました！）はなぜ海賊になったのでしょう．英語本文ではこれらの点を検討し，最後に歴史上の海賊と我々の知るカリブの海賊イメージとの関係についても考えてみたいと思います．

研究の素材

　では，歴史上の海賊は何をもとに研究できるのでしょうか．歴史学の場合，研究の素材となるのは「一次史料」と呼ばれるものです．これは平たく言えば，自分が調べたいと思っている時代，あるいはそれに近い時代に書かれた記録です．一方，一次史料をもとに後代の歴史家が書いた本や論文は，「二次文献」と呼ばれています．

　一次史料は歴史家にとって，実際には行くことのできない過去の世界を垣間見ることのできる「窓」として重要なものです．何が一次史料になるかは調べたい対象にもよりますが，基本的には書かれた記録であれば何でも一次史料になりえます．例えば政府文書，会計記録，個人の手紙，当時の新聞などです．最近では絵画などの図像資料や発掘されたモノなどの考古学的史料，インタビュー記録なども援用されることがあります．

　では，海賊を研究する場合の一次史料にはどのようなものがあるのでしょうか．実は海賊自身が残した記録というのはあまりありません．例外的に17世紀後半に南米太平洋岸に進出した海賊の中には航海記を出版した者もいますが，本章で扱う18世紀初頭の「黄金時代」の海賊は社会のはずれ者的存在であるため，そもそも記録を書き残さないか，あるいは書いていてもそれが残っていることはきわめて稀です．そのため，この時代の海賊に関する史料は，海賊自身ではなく他の人々が書き記したものが中心になります．

　まず挙げられるのは，海賊を取り締まる公権力側の史料です．具体的にはイギ

リス本国や植民地の諸機関の史料，あるいは裁判記録などです．しかし，これらはあくまで海賊を鎮圧する側の視点に立って書かれた史料であるため，これだけでは海賊の姿は一面的なものになってしまいます．

　一方，海賊について第三者が記した記録もあります．18世紀初頭でとりわけ有名なのは，チャールズ・ジョンソンなる人物によって書かれた，当時の海賊についての一種のルポルタージュである『もっとも悪名高い海賊たちによる強盗と殺人の全史』という著作です（ただし，この本には創作と思われる部分も少なくないため，史料として使う際には注意が必要です）．また他にも，当時の人々の海賊イメージを明らかにしたいのであれば，同時代の文学作品や演劇なども分析対象となるでしょう．

研究の楽しさ

　このような一次史料を通して，海賊を含めた過去の人々の生きざまや思想，さらにはそれを取り巻く当時の社会や政治，経済のあり方を明らかにすることには，小説や映画のようなフィクションを鑑賞するのとはまた違う面白さがあります．日々生きていれば誰でも感じるように，現実の世界は小説や映画のようにドラマチックではありませんし，カタルシスを与えてくれるわけでもありません．登場するのも偉人や成功者ばかりではありません．本章で扱う大半の海賊のように日陰の身のまま一生を終わる人も多くいます．また善意や愛や高潔さだけでなく，悪意や憎しみや凡庸な卑劣さにも満ち満ちているのが現実の世界です．人々を取り巻く社会や国家も，決して個人のことを親身に考えてくれるわけではありません．時代の流れや政治の動きに人々の人生が無情にすり潰される光景を，我々は日々目にしているはずです．それは過去の世界も同じです．

　しかし，非情ともいえる歴史の流れに翻弄されながら，また時にはじたばたと格好の悪い面も見せながら，何とかもがいて生きていた人々の姿，いわば過去の人々の生の姿が史料を通して垣間見えたときには，でき合いの英雄譚や美談にはないリアリティを感じることができます．さらに人々の行為だけでなく，人々がなぜそういう人生をたどることになったのか，その歴史的背景となる当時の社会や政治，経済の構造やその変動を理解することからは，フィクションを観たり読んだりしてワクワクするのとはまた違った，静かで深い知的興奮が得られるのです．

研究がめざすこと

　このように歴史研究は，過去に生きた人々の行為や思想，さらにはそれを取り巻く政治・社会・経済的構造の解明をめざします．では，それにはどのような意味があるのでしょうか．人種差別のような現代の重要な問題にも直接つながる歴史を扱う場合は，その遠因を明らかにするという意味があると言えそうです．ではカリブの海賊のように一見現代とは関係のない対象を研究することには，知的好奇心を満たす以外に，一体どのような意義があると言えるのでしょうか．

　まず挙げられるのは，歴史学は政治，経済，社会，文化などの幅広い文脈の中で対象をとらえる見方を教えてくれるということです．過去の世界のある事象を理解するには，その事象だけに注目していてはわかりません．一見些細な問題でも，より広い文脈の中で考えて，初めてその重要性を理解できることもしばしばだからです．例えば本章で見る 18 世紀初頭の海賊の問題も，当時のイギリス政府にとっては通商の安全確保の問題，植民地貿易に従事する商人にとっては経済問題であり，また時には自ら海賊にも加わった商船の水夫たちにとっては，一種の労働問題の性格も帯びていました．このように問題をさまざまな観点から見ることの重要性は現代の現象の分析にも言えることですが，歴史学の場合は特に，対象が置かれた文脈の歴史的固有性を意識することも求められます．過去の現象を理解するには，それを現代の価値観だけで判断しようとはせずに，それを取り巻く当時の状況や諸条件の，今との違いにも敏感になる必要があるのです．

　このように，歴史研究の意義は，今我々が生きている世界とは異なる世界の，固有のあり方に対する繊細な感覚をもちつつ，対象となる事象を幅広い文脈の中で分析する思考法を学べる点にもあると言えます．それはまた，現代についての理解を深めることにもつながります．歴史研究を通じて，過去の世界のあり方や価値観の思わぬ異質や共通点に触れることは，知らず知らずのうちに凝り固まっていた我々の認識の枠組みをゆるめ解きほぐして，より広い視野で我々の生きる世界をとらえることを可能にしてくれるのです．

Pirates of the Caribbean: Their Images and Realities

TABLE OF CONTENTS

4. Activities of the Pirates and Their Suppression

5. Conclusion

1. Introduction

When people hear the word 'pirate', they might have many different images in their mind. Some might think of the Vikings in Scandinavia, the *Wako* in East Asia, or perhaps the *Murakami-Suigun* in Japan. However, many people would also think of the pirates of the Caribbean. The image of the pirates with a dreadful black beard, a hook hand, and an eye-patch became very popular among many people through various media, such as novels, Hollywood films, and comic books. In these fictional stories, pirates are sometimes depicted as kind of anti-heroes who were rough and wild but loved freedom and fought against an oppressive government and established hierarchy of the society. However, this image does not reflect the real pirates who lived in the past.

In terms of their appearance, the pirates in fictions were modelled mainly on pirates in the late seventeenth and early eighteenth centuries. In particular, it was the pirates who appeared in the Caribbean and North America in the period after the War of Spanish Succession (1702-1714) that formed our image of pirates. This period, which is often called the 'Golden Age of Piracy' (1716-1726), produced some of the most famous pirates in European and American history, such as Edward Teach (Blackbeard) and Bartholomew

Figure 1   Bartholomew Roberts, one of the most powerful pirates in the 'Golden Age of Piracy' [Captain Charles Johnson, *A General History of the Robberies and Murders of the Most Notorious Pyrates* (London, 1724)]

Roberts (see Figure 1).

Their images are familiar to many of us, but their real lives and activities, which studies on the social history of pirates have revealed, are not well known. The latter might not be as romantic and dramatic as the lives of the pirates in fiction, but they are equally interesting and can provide us with an insight into the struggles of the real people living in the past. Who were they? Why did they become pirates? What was their purpose? In the following sections, relying on recent historical studies on pirates, this chapter tries to answer these questions.

2. The 'Golden Age of Piracy'

Marcus Rediker, one of the leading scholars of the history of early modern British piracy, estimated that there were, roughly speaking, about 4,000 pirates in total during the 'Golden Age'. Even when we limit the number to those operating in one year, it is estimated to be from 1,000 to 2,000.[1] Readers might wonder whether this number is large or not, but it should be pointed out that the number of seamen serving in the British Navy in this period was about 13,000. It should be also remembered that New York, the largest city in North America, had a population of only about 18,000 around the same time, and Port Royal in Jamaica, the largest city in the Caribbean, had a population of only about 3,000. When these figures are taken into account, it would be easy to imagine what a threat a few thousand pirates could pose to people at the time, especially those living in European colonies in North America and the Caribbean.[2] These pirates were also very active. Rediker estimates that about 2,400 ships were captured by them during this period.[3] Thus, during the 'Golden Age of Piracy', merchant vessels sailing in the Atlantic as well as other oceans in the world were under a serious and continuous threat from these roaming sea bandits.

However, it should be also stressed that this was almost the last large-scale outbreak of piracy in which European and American pirates played an

---

1   Marcus Rediker, *Villains of All Nations: Atlantic Pirates in the Golden Age* (Boston: Beacon Press, 2004), 9, 29.

2   Rediker, 2004, 30; David Cordingly, *Under the Black Flag: The Romance and the Reality of Life among the Pirates* (New York: Random House, 1996, repr. San Diego, CA: Harcourt Brace & Company, 1997), 202.

3   Rediker, 2004, 33.

important role. Therefore, it might not be entirely correct to call this period the 'Golden Age'. It was, in fact, the final stage of the history of European and American piracy, which was disappearing in the face of increasing control and suppression of maritime plunder by European governments.

Why, then, did a large number of the pirates appear in this period? The direct cause was relatively clear: the shipwreck of a Spanish silver fleet off the coast of Florida. A silver fleet was a group of ships whose task was to bring back silver and other American products from Spanish American colonies to Spain and to carry European goods to those colonies. In July 1715, one of these fleets met a hurricane off the Florida coast and was wrecked with a large amount of treasure, such as silver and gold.

Although the ships were sunk, even with the technology at the time, it was not impossible to salvage some of their sunken cargo with the assistance of divers, and the Spaniards soon started to rescue valuable goods from the wrecks. However, unfortunately for them, one Captain Henry Jennings, an ex-privateer captain in Jamaica, learned this news. 'Privateers' were ships (or people) allowed by their own government to seize enemy merchant ships in war time. This might sound like an act of piracy, but, in early modern Europe, as long as the privateers observed the rules set by the government, this was regarded as a legitimate practice. However, privateering was allowed only in war time. Therefore, when the war of Spanish Succession ended, many privateers lost their jobs, and Jennings was one of them.

When Jennings heard about the shipwreck, he decided to seize the rich cargo, and, with his men, he attacked the Spaniards engaged in the salvage, robbing them of the treasure, and returned to Jamaica. Since the war with Spain had already ended, this was not a legal act of privateering, but an act of piracy, and therefore attracted strong protests from the Spanish governor in Cuba. In fear of being punished, Jennings and his men fled to New Providence Island in the Bahamas, a half-abandoned British colony, and established their base there. Thereafter, they attracted more and more people, who joined their gang.

These people who became members of the pirates in the early stage of the 'Golden Age' can be divided mainly into two groups: ex-privateers like Jennings who wanted to continue plundering even after the war ended, and logwood cutters, who were engaged in cutting logwood (wood use in creating fabric dyes) in the jungles of Central America but were expelled by the

Spaniards and lost their jobs.

However, these unemployed people were not the only sources of pirates. Soon, another group began to join them. According to Rediker, many of the pirates in this period were not the unemployed. They were originally sailors working on board English merchant ships that were attacked by pirates. After their ships were taken, some of the sailors decided to join the pirates. What drove them into a life of piracy was not unemployment, but other economic factors: decrease of wages and ill treatment of seamen.

Seamen in the eighteenth century had tough job with many dangers involved in life at sea. In war time, however, there were some advantages for them. Because of the shortage of seamen caused by soaring demand in the navy, their wages were often increased up to 30, or sometimes to 50 shillings per lunar month. However, once war ended, wages were usually reduced to about 24 to 25 shillings. This was also the case for the period after the War of Spanish Succession. Moreover, in 1715, an economic depression set in. In addition, during the eighteenth century, discipline on board merchant ships was increasingly becoming harsher. These changes made works on board merchant ships almost unbearable for many seamen, which often induced them to join pirates.[4] Thus, in this period, the number of pirates rapidly grew, absorbing those seamen dissatisfied with their working conditions.

3. Real Pirates of the Caribbean and Their Communities

In terms of their place of birth, as Rediker's analysis shows, these pirates were mainly from the British Isles, which include the islands of Great Britain and Ireland (See Figure 2). Nearly half of them (47.4%) were from England, followed by those from Ireland (9.8%), Scotland (6.3%), and Wales (4.0%). Also, people from British colonies in North America and the Caribbean account for about one fourth of the total. In addition, there was a small number

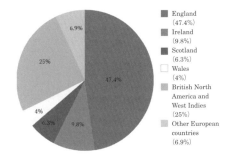

Figure 2 Place of birth
[Source: Rediker, 2004]

---

4   Rediker, 2004, 23-24, 42-43.

of seamen from other countries, such as the Netherlands, France and Portugal (6.9%). All in all, the majority of the pirates in this period were from the British Isles or British colonies in America. It should be also pointed out that the pirates in this period included some people of African origins, who were ex-slaves or free blacks, as well as a small number of Native Americans.[5]

In terms of their age, the average was 28.2 years old. By the standard of the time, this means that they were seamen with some experience at sea. Most of them were single, and in terms of their social class, they were from the lowest rank of the social hierarchy.[6]

Although the vast majority of the pirates were male, there were, in fact, a few female pirates too. The most famous ones were Ann Bonny and Mary Read, who were members of the gang of John Rackham, alias Calico Jack. In late 1720, they were captured and were put on trial. The two female pirates became famous because their biography was recorded in A General History of the Pyrates (1724), a widely read non-fiction account of the pirates at the time, written by one Captain Charles Johnson.[7] Although the credibility of most of their biography is doubted, the fact that these two female pirates existed can be confirmed by other sources, such as an account of their trials. They were sentenced to death, but their execution was postponed because they were pregnant. Read died in jail, but Bonny's fate remains unknown.

Regarding the communities of the pirates made up of the abovementioned people, there is one aspect that is often stressed by historians: their 'egalitarian' and 'democratic' characters. There are several reasons for this emphasis. First of all, power-relations in pirate ships were very different from other contemporary ships, such as naval ships and merchant ships. In pirate ships, captains were chosen by the whole crew, while the captains of the naval and merchant ships were chosen by the Admiralty (the British government department in charge of the naval affairs), or by ship owners, and the ship's crew had virtually no say in the choice. Furthermore, unlike the latter ships, where captains (or masters) often had absolute power over their men, the

---

5   Rediker, 2004, 50–56; Peter Earle, The Pirate Wars (London: Methuen Publishing, 2004), 170–72.

6   Rediker, 2004, 49–50.

7   Captain Charles Johnson, A General History of the Robberies and Murders of the Most Notorious Pyrates, with introduction and commentary by David Cordingly (London: Conway Maritime Press, 1998, repr. Guilford, CT: Lyons Press, 2002), 117–31.

power of pirate captains was generally limited, except when they were in pursuit of their prey or in a battle. Important decisions affecting the entire crew—for example, the next destination or punishment to be given to those violating the rules of the ships—were often made by a majority vote, a practice which was almost unthinkable in naval and merchant ships at the time. Moreover, in pirate ships, the power of the captains was usually restricted by the presence of 'quartermasters', a person or persons who acted as a representative of the whole crew. The ultimate power in pirate ships lay not with captains but with the 'common council', i.e., a general meeting of the whole company of the ship. It was in this meeting where captains as well as quartermasters were chosen and where important decisions were made. If captains or quartermasters were thought to be unqualified, they might be even expelled by the common council.[8]

These 'egalitarian' and 'democratic' characteristics of pirate communities can be seen in the 'pirates' articles', i.e., rules which pirates established when forming a new party. In particular, these characteristics were noticeable in a rule of distribution of booty, or treasure and goods stolen by pirates. Ordinary members of pirate ships were usually entitled to one share. On the other hand, captains and quartermasters could receive one and half to two shares, while sailors with special skills, such as boatswains and carpenters, could also receive one and quarter to one and half share. Indeed, there was a gap between ordinary members and captains in terms of their shares, but this gap was far smaller than in naval ships where captains sometimes could receive a hundred times more shares of prize money than ordinary seamen. In addition, members of pirate ships could receive sufficient compensation when they were injured during a battle, which is equivalent to compensation for a worker accident in the modern era.[9] Thus, it can be said that, in many respects, pirates could enjoy power and rights which other contemporary seamen did not have.

4. Activities of the Pirates and Their Suppression

People tend to imagine that pirates were reckless and bold people. However, in reality, this was not the case. The pirates in this period tried to avoid

---

8 Rediker, 2004, 65-70.
9 Rediker, 2004, 70, 73-74.

unnecessary fights as much as possible. This is simply because their aim was usually not a fight but money. Their favourite tactic was to use threats. When they found a possible target, they approached it, firing guns and flying a pirate flag. This was mainly intended to intimidate the target and cow them into submission, attempts in which they often succeeded. A famous pirate flag with the skull and crossbones called the 'Jolly Roger' was, in fact, a tool for this tactic of intimidation, as well as a symbol of their gang.

One of the reasons their tactic was so successful was the sheer number of the crew. Small merchant ships, a common prey for pirates, usually had only 10 to 20 men on board them. By contrast, pirate ships of a similar size often had 150 to 200 men. Because of this differential, once overtaken, crew in merchant ships were no match for pirates, and they often soon surrendered.

Pirate ships usually had many guns on board them. However, unlike pirates in films and comic books, they tended to hesitate to fire them directly at their target ship. The reason is simple. They did not want to see their prey destroyed by their cannonballs and sunk in the sea with its cargoes. Pirates themselves were often heavily armed too, but, if they were able to obtain treasure without bloodshed, they preferred it. However, this does not mean that pirates were peace-loving people. They sometimes exerted violence mercilessly—if necessary, for example, to extract information about booty from captives, or to take revenge for their comrades killed by the navy.[10]

Another aspect of the pirates' behaviour different from those in fictions was that they rarely buried their treasures, except for a few notable cases. Unlike pirates in earlier periods, the pirates in this period were always faced with the fear of being captured and hanged or killed during fights with the navy. For the people always living with this grim prospect, there was really no point in hiding their treasures. They preferred to spend it on drinking and women while they were still alive and could enjoy their lives.[11] The life of pirates in this period was, indeed, harsh and short.

During the 'Golden Age of Piracy', pirates attacked merchant vessels almost all over the world: North American waters, the Caribbean, the West African coasts, the Indian Ocean, Red Sea, and Persian Gulf. However, it was not long before operations to suppress these pirates were started by European

---

10 Cordingly, 1996, 106-7, 114-16, 119-20, 129-30, 202; Rediker, 2004, 14-15.
11 Cordingly, 1996, 179.

governments, especially the British government. In fact, similar attempts at suppression had existed before, but it was not until this period that the operations achieved remarkable success.

Some pirates were killed in fights with the navy and privateers, while others were captured. When they were captured, the fate often awaiting them was a death sentence (usually, hanging), though there were some cases in which they were pardoned just before the execution. If they were executed in England, their body was hanged for a while at Wapping on the north bank of the River Thames in London, and, if the person executed was a notorious pirate, the body was hanged at a more visible place, as an example to sailors sailing up and down the river, lest they should think of turning into pirates.[12]

Because of the active anti-piracy operations by the navy and colonists, the pirates were largely suppressed by around 1726, or at the latest, around 1730. Thereafter, occasional cases of piracy still happened from time to time, but, as far as the piracy conducted by Europeans were concerned, large-scale outbreaks of piracy ceased to be a serious problem for European shipping.

5. Conclusion

Pirates in films and comic books are often depicted as brave and freedom-loving people. However, as we have seen, historical studies have revealed that real pirates living in the past were somewhat different from their image in fiction. The majority of the pirates in the period after the War of Spanish Succession were, in fact, seamen who joined a gang of pirates because of unemployment and deterioration of their working conditions. Thus, in many cases, real pirates were not romantic anti-heroes, but seamen driven into a life of piracy by their desperate economic conditions.

Here, people might wonder how these pirates, poor and desperate sailors, came to be fictionalized as romantic anti-heroes. The historical process of the idealisation of pirates and the creation of this romantic image has yet to be examined, but it should be pointed out that this kind of idealisation had already begun in the early eighteenth century when piracy was still rampant. In the second volume of *A General History of the Pyrates*, Captain Johnson wrote about 'Libertalia', a pirate commonwealth reputedly established by one Captain Misson, a French pirate, and Caraccioli, an Italian priest. 'Libertalia'

---

12 Cordingly, 1996, 223–25.

was claimed to have been a free and egalitarian society, where all properties were shared and where slavery was abolished.[13] In fact, its existence is doubted, since there was no other evidence to prove it. It is more likely that 'Libertalia' was a fiction that represented a radical criticism of mainstream society at the time, or reflected a utopian ideal of which some people then dreamed.

It was likely that this process of idealisation accelerated after pirates ceased to be a real threat to people in Europe and in America. In this process, people probably projected various ideals and political ideologies upon pirates in history. In a sense, historical pirates plundering at sea functioned as a kind of a mirror which reflected ideas or desires of the people living on land. We can still see this process in modern fictions about pirates, such as Captain Jack Sparrow in the *Pirates of the Caribbean* and Luffy in *One Piece*. This process of idealisation could be a good subject of historical studies too. We can investigate not only the reality of pirates, but also how people have perceived them; in other words, we can investigate the history of people's images of and ideas about pirates.

Nowadays, pirates have reappeared in some places in the world, such as Indonesia and Somalia. Therefore, it is possible that our image of pirates might change again in the future, reflecting the change in our reality, and this could be another topic for further historical studies.

▌ References

Cordingly, David. *Under the Black Flag: The Romance and the Reality of Life among the Pirates.* New York: Random House, 1996; San Diego, CA: Harcourt Brace & Company, 1997.

Earle, Peter, *The Pirate Wars.* London: Methuen Publishing, 2004.

Johnson, Captain Charles, *A General History of the Robberies and Murders of the Most Notorious Pyrates,* with introduction and commentary by David Cordingly. London: Conway Maritime Press, 1998; Guilford, CT: Lyons Press, 2002.

Rediker, Marcus, 'Libertalia: The Pirate's Utopia'. In *Pirates: Terror on the High Seas from the Caribbean to the South China Sea.* Edited by David

---

13　For Libertalia, see Marcus Rediker, 'Libertalia: The Pirate's Utopia,' in David Cordingly (ed.), *Pirates: Terror on the High Seas from the Caribbean to the South China Sea* (Atlanta: Turner Publications, 1996).

Cordingly, Atlanta: Turner Publishing, 1996.

Rediker, Marcus, *Villains of All Nations: Atlantic Pirates in the Golden Age*. Boston: Beacon Press, 2004.

Further Reading

Cordingly, David. *Seafaring Women: Adventures of Pirate Queens, Female Stowaways, and Sailors' Wives*. New York: Random House, 2001.

Ritchie, Robert C., *Captain Kidd and the War against the Pirates*. Cambridge, MA: Harvard University Press, 1986.

日本語文献案内

金澤周作編『海のイギリス史：闘争と共生の世界史』昭和堂，2013 年.

薩摩真介『〈海賊〉の大英帝国：掠奪と交易の四百年史』講談社選書メチエ，2018 年.

考えてみよう

　「海賊」のように，そのイメージやとらえ方が時代によって大きく変化した歴史上の存在や出来事には，他にどのようなものがあるか考えてみよう．また，そのようにイメージが大きく変わった背景は何であったのかも考えてみよう.

・・

薩摩　真介
Shinsuke SATSUMA

ことばのしくみ研究

Building Blocks of Words and Sentences:
A Comparative Study between English and Japanese

概要

　言語学は「ことば」を対象とする学問ですが，言語学の中には言語と社会との関わりを研究する社会言語学（9章）や言語の歴史を研究する歴史言語学，言語獲得や言語処理（言語の産出・理解）のメカニズム解明に取り組む心理言語学など，学問領域は多岐に渡り，各分野の研究対象や研究目的も大きく異なります.

　本章では，言語を構成する規則・原理，すなわち「ことばのしくみ」を明らかにすることを目的とする理論言語学（生成文法）という学問を紹介します. また，理論言語学の中でも生成文法という分野の考えに基づき，言語をヒトに固有の言語能力（知識）とみなし，ヒトは言語を獲得する能力を生得的に備えているという立場からことばにアプローチします.

国際英語文化の中の言語理論研究

　「国際英語文化」という語から皆さんはどのような意味を想像するでしょうか. 「国際英語」の「文化」というような意味をおそらく考えたのではないでしょうか.

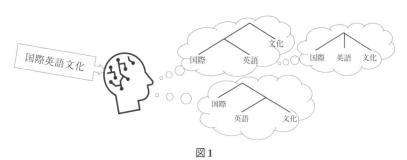

図1

あるいは「国際」的な「英語文化」という意味を想像したでしょうか．いずれにしても，「国際英語文化」が何を意味するのかは抽象的ではっきりとしないかもしれません．ですが，これらの具体的な意味はさておき，「国際英語文化」が「国際文化」の「英語」という意味や，「国際文化」と「英語」という意味にはならないことは，（「国際文化」が何であるかはさておき）直感的にわかるはずです．このように，私たちは言語に対する直感を無意識のレベルでもっています．本章の言語理論研究が基盤とする生成文法理論は，この直感のことを言語能力あるいは言語知識と呼び，言語を英語や日本語といった具体的なものではなく，ヒトに固有の言語能力，つまり私たちのもつ「母語の知識」という抽象的な概念としてとらえています．

　ここで，「国際英語」という語が，今日の社会で用いられる文脈ないしは環境や意味を考えると，これまでのような実態的かつ具体的な英語という言語ではなく，さまざまな社会的・地位的変種を含む，より抽象的で多様なレベルの言語がそこには想定されていることがわかります．コミュニケーションの手段としての国際英語は上で述べた生成文法理論が定義する言語の概念やそれが用いられる文脈からは大きく解離します．一方，個別言語のレベルでも，従来の認識であった「英語」という，ある種の具体的な概念を国際英語という，より抽象的な概念としてとらえ直すことが，今日の社会においても起きていることがわかるのです．

研究の楽しさ

　言語理論研究の魅力とは，一体何だと皆さんは思いますか．理論という語からは少し難解なイメージを抱くかもしれませんが，言語，つまり，ことば自体は身近に感じるでしょう．言語理論研究とは，平たく言えば「ことばのしくみ」を考えることです．ただし，この「ことば」という語の指す意味には注意が必要で，上でも述べた通り，生成文法理論という理論言語学の分野は言語を英語や日本語といった個別言語としてではなく，〈ヒトに固有の言語能力といった抽象的な概念〉としてとらえています．ここが重要なところです．それでは，この言語能力とは一体どのようなものなのでしょうか．

　言語能力とは別の言い方をすれば，言語に関し，私たちが無意識に有する知識を意味します．この「無意識に」というところがポイントなのですが，この点について，次の造語を用いて考えてみましょう．日本語に「らみ」という架空の語があったとします．この語が，「らみが見つからない」という文に現れると，「らみ」は何かの指示物を示す名詞であることがわかります．一方で，「今日，らみったよ」という文においては，「らみ」は動詞として分析されます．そして，「今日，

らみ（ら）なかった」という否定形は作れますが,「今日, らみ（ら）ないかった」とはならないこともわかります. 一方で,「らみのらみが, らみがらみったと思っていると, らみのらみのらみが言ってたよ」といった具合に,「らみ」を用いてより複雑な名詞句をつくることも, 文を好きなだけ長くすることも私たちにはできるのです[1]. このように, 私たちは「らみ」の意味が何かを知らずとも, 名詞や動詞と言われるものがどういう形をもち, どのような環境に起こるのかを知っており, また, 文を無限に長くすることができることを無意識に知っています. そして, この無意識の知識を用いて新たな語を創造し, 理解することができます.

　本セクションの締めくくりとして, 酒井（2019：51）で紹介されている次の例を最後に考察してみましょう.「花子が太郎に自分の写真を見せた」と言ったときの「自分」は,「花子」のみを指すのに対し,「花子が太郎に自分の写真を撮らせた」と言うと,「自分」は「花子」も「太郎」のどちらも指すことができます. 母語について, みなさんはこのような知識を身につけているのだということを, ご存じでしたか. 言語研究の楽しさは, まさにこの「無意識の知識」に気づいたときのゾワゾワっとする高揚感や, その知識を通して言語の本質を知りたいという知的好奇心が感じられる瞬間にあると思います.

この章のトピック

　本章では, ことばのしくみの中でも特に語や文の仕組みについて触れます. 語とは何かということを定義するのは非常に難しい問題なのですが, 語の仕組みを扱う形態論（morphology）という分野では,「単独で起こり得る最小の単位」として語を定義しています. 例えば,「お皿」という語において,「皿」は語として成り立ちますが,「お」は単独で成り立たないため,「お」は語ではないことになります. また, 語は更に句という単位を形成します. 例えば, *drink* と *coffee* という語を組み合わせると, *drink coffee* という動詞句が形成されます. 更に, 句は文を形成します. 本章では, まず初めに語がどのような規則に基づいて形成されるのかについて, 語形成というプロセスを考察します. 次に, 統語論（syntax）という分野における, 句や文の構造について考察します. そして, 語と句や文の構造を介して言語に共通する原理を探ります.

1　酒井（2019：215）が『チョムスキーと言語脳科学』において, ルイス・キャロルの『鏡の国のアリス』で使用された「ジャバウォッキー文」について言及しています. これを日本語に応用した例では, 動詞の活用と助詞以外は完全に無意味な語が並べられた文となっていますが, 日本語の統語構造が維持されていることがわかります.

研究の素材

　本章で紹介する生成文法（generative grammar）理論はヒトの言語能力を明らかにすることを目標としていることから，研究素材となるのは，私たちヒトが生み出す言語データです．ただし，言語データは日常生活における会話や本・テレビなどから抽出するのではなく，任意の言語理論を検証するために自ら作り出す必要があります．先ほど引用した「らみのらみが，らみがらみったと思っていると，らみのらみのらみが言ってたよ」などの文はそれにあたります．また，言語データの中には文法的なデータのみならず，論理的には生成可能であるにもかかわらず非文法的なデータも含まれます．もちろん，本章で後ほど紹介する「うれしみ」などといった SNS などを源とするデータを観察することもありますが，その際にも「うれしみ」がどのような文法的環境に現れ得るのかを確かめるために，さまざまな環境要因を考慮しデータをさらに構築することが必要です．したがって，生成文法が研究素材とするデータは日常生活では用いられることのない，「変な」語や文が多いことが特徴です．

研究がめざすこと

　本章の言語理論研究が基盤とする生成文法理論は，アメリカの言語学者である，ノーム・チョムスキー（1928-）によって 1950 年代に提唱されました．上で述べたように，生成文法理論は言語を英語や日本語といった具体的な存在物ではなく，ヒトに固有の言語能力（言語の知識）といった抽象的な概念としてとらえています[2]．したがって，言語研究とは，私たちがもつ言語能力ないしは言語知識の研究を意味することになります．

　生成文法が従来の言語学と大きく異なる点は，私たちはこの言語能力を学習や模倣などによって後天的に身につけたのではなく，生まれながらに脳に備えているという仮説を立てていることです．ここで注意しなければならないのは，チョムスキーは私たちが日本語なり英語なりの個別文法の知識や運用能力を生まれながらにしてもつと言っているのではなく，「母語を獲得する能力（システム）」を生得的に有していると言っていることです[3]．したがって，生成文法は言語を脳

2　チョムスキー（2011）（福井直樹・辻子美保子訳）『生成文法の企て』においても，訳者が「言語」という概念の定義について強調しています．

3　この点については，酒井（2019）が『チョムスキーと言語脳科学』において，脳科学者としての立場から生成文法理論の立場を明快に述べています．

116

（心）に内在化された自然物としてとらえ，言語学を自然科学の対象としている点で，他の言語学とは異なる立場をとっています（福井，2001；酒井，2002 他）．生成文法では，この母語を獲得する能力を普遍文法（universal grammar）と呼び，普遍文法はヒトに固有でかつ普遍的であるという仮説を立てています．そして，この普遍文法の解明を究極的にはめざしています [4].

　このような仮説を立てる背景には，「人間が限られた（言語）経験から経験以上の知識をどのようにして得るのか」という，プラトンの問題（Plato's problem）と呼ばれる問いがあります．幼児は驚くべきスピードで母語を獲得しますが，「無意識の知識」で見たように，子どもは耳に入ってくる言語データ以上の知識を有しています．また，子どもが触れるデータは大人の言い間違いなど「不完全」なデータを多く含むにもかかわらず，誰もが問題なく母語をマスターします．「研究の楽しさ」で見た，私たちのもつ言語に対する「直感」は，学校などで意識的に学んで得たものではありません．私たちは明示的に母語の文法を教わることなく，創造的にことばを産み出し，また理解することができます．この能力こそが，人間の本質であると生成文法は考え，その詳細を研究において解明しようとしているのです．

Building Blocks of Words and Sentences:
A Comparative Study between English and Japanese

TABLE OF CONTENTS

1.　Introduction

　Our ability as children to acquire complex and structured language, demonstrating that we know how language works without being explicitly taught, is truly a marvelous characteristic of being human. According to Noam Chom-

---

4　「普遍文法」はヒトの言語能力（生まれて間もない，他の言語データに一切さらされていない初期状態）そのものを指す場合とその言語能力を説明する理論を指す場合があり，多義性をもちます．この点については，チョムスキー（2017）（福井直樹・辻子美保子訳）『統辞理論の諸相：方法論序説』の「五十周年記念版への序説」でも明示されています．

sky, an American linguist and a proponent of the linguistic theory called *generative grammar*, our knowledge of language is innate; that is, we are born with the ability to learn and use language. Chomsky's theory provides us with a clue to understanding how babies, in principle, can acquire any natural language they are exposed to and to become masters of that language. This chapter discusses some aspects of that linguistic knowledge that we use but are not aware of, focusing on our tacit knowledge about words and sentences.

The organization of the chapter is as follows. Section 2 briefly introduces the branches of linguistics, especially in the field of theoretical linguistics. Section 3 describes some aspects of word formation and its rules, an area of study called *morphology*. Section 4 discusses some of the sentence formation and its rules, known as *syntax*, and section 5 concludes this chapter.

2.　The Branch of Theoretical Linguistics

What is a language made of? Words? Sentences? While both words and sentences are indeed units of a language, they can be broken down into smaller linguistic units called *morphemes*: a morpheme is the smallest unit of linguistic meaning. When a morpheme can stand alone, it constitutes a word by itself (e.g. 'desk', 'walk', 'small', 'on', 'very'), but some morphemes are *bound morphemes* and cannot appear alone but must be attached to another morpheme to be realised as part of a word (e.g. 'unhappy', 'walks', 'smaller', where bound morphemes are underlined). As will be described in section 3, how morphemes are assembled into a word is not randomly decided but is regulated by rules. The area of linguistics that studies the structure of words and rules of word formation is called morphology.

A morpheme can be further broken down into speech sounds, namely *consonants* and *vowels*. For example, the word 'unhappy' is made of two morphemes, 'un-' and 'happy', and each consists of a set of sounds: [ən] and [hæpi].[5] Similar to how morphemes are combined to form words, sounds also group together according to rules. The study of speech sound patterns is called *phonology*, which is a branch of theoretical linguistics.

When words are assembled together, larger linguistic units called *phrases*

5　The symbols in square brackets are from the International Phonetic Alphabet (IPA), where each symbol uniquely describes how (e.g. by using the tongue, by completely stopping the airflow, etc.) and where (e.g. in the mouth, with the lips, teeth, etc.) a given sound is produced.

can be formed. For example, grouping together the words 'eat' and 'apples' creates a verb phrase [vp eat apples].⁶ When a VP is combined with a subject noun phrase (NP), it can form a sentence. As will be seen in more detail in section 4, the study of phrase and sentence structure is called *syntax*, and sentence formation is also regulated by a set of rules.

All words, phrases, and sentences are associated with meaning, and the study of meaning in language is called *semantics*. Although semantics is not covered in this chapter, there is a strict correlation between morphological/ syntactic structure and the corresponding meaning. In addition, it should be noted that semantics only refers to the literal meaning of a given word, phrase, or sentence, and the contribution to meaning from the situation or context of utterances is outside the scope of semantics. Context-dependent meaning, like background information about the speaker, hearer, and situation of a given utterance, is the focus of the study called *pragmatics*, which is often set aside from the core branch of theoretical linguistics.

Although all the areas of linguistics mentioned above are equally important, the focus of this chapter will be on morphology and syntax, as the fundamental components of the grammar of a language. Furthermore, English and Japanese will be used as examples so that our (near) native intuitions about these languages will guide us to a better understanding of our tacit knowledge about language.

3. Morphology: A Study of Words

As briefly mentioned in section 2, a word is assembled according to rules of word formation. For example, the suffix morphemes '-ity' and '-ness' both create nouns by attaching to a morphological unit called a *base* in the adjective category. The base could be one morpheme or multiple morphemes grouped together (see Siegel 1974, Aronoff 1976, and Selkirk 1982 for the different morpho-phonological properties of *-ity* and *-ness* affixation).⁷ When '-ity' is affixed to the adjective 'curious' it yields the derived noun 'curiosity'. In linguistics, the rule that regulates how linguistic units are combined is called *selection*. Note that '-ity' must select adjectives and cannot attach to

---

6   The square brackets indicate that the relevant string of words form a phrasal unit and the label VP specifies it as a verb phrase.

7   Affixation refers to the attaching of a 'suffix' or 'prefix' to a morphological base.

other parts of speech. For instance, an attempt to make a derived noun like *'understandity' out of the verb 'understand' fails.[8]

It is not the case, however, that '-ity' can be attached to every adjective: for instance, the adjective 'glorious' cannot be made into the derived noun *'gloriousity', but the noun derived by attaching '-ness' giving 'gloriousness' is allowed (Aronoff 1976, Embick & Marantz 2008). Interestingly, the adjective 'curious'can also be made into the noun 'curiousness (*Ibid.*)'. In fact, -'ness' has much wider distribution than '-ity', since it can attach to a wider range of adjectives. Thus, it is said to be more *productive*, in linguistics terms, than '-ity', which has more restrictions on its attaching adjective.

The morphological structures of these derived nouns can be represented roughly like (1a, b) and (2a, b), and (3).[9]

In the structures above, the label A stands for adjectives, N for nouns, V for verbs, and Af for affixes. Each structure is interpreted as the affix selecting, correctly or incorrectly, the base next to it on the bottom layer (i.e. an adjective in (1a,b) and (2a,b), and a verb in (3)). And on the top layer, the category of the derived word is successfully or unsuccessfully assigned (i.e. in all

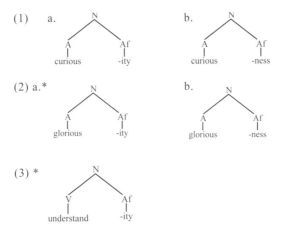

---

8   The symbol '*' indicates that the relevant word formation is ungrammatical.

9   Note that Embick & Marantz (2008) propose different structures for the *-ity* and *-ness* adjectives. The difference in productivity of these two affixes and their corresponding structural positions are ignored for simplicity.

of the examples above, the (intended) assigned category is a noun).

Let us now look at what seem to be similar examples in Japanese with the morphemes -*mi* and -*sa,* both of which select adjectives and create nouns. For example, -*mi* can yield the derived noun 甘み *ama-mi* 'sweetness' by attaching to the adjective 甘い *ama(-i)* 'sweet', and -*sa* can also yield the derived noun 甘さ *ama-sa* 'sweetness' from the same adjective. Like the English '-ity', however, -*mi* is more selective than -*sa* about its selected adjective (Kageyama 1993, Sugioka 2005, Morita 2018). For example, 静かさ *sizuka-sa* 'quietness' is a properly derived noun, since -*sa* can select the adjective 静か *shizuka* 'quiet', but * 静かみ **sizuka-mi* is not a grammatical form (Sugioka 2005：77). This type of data shows that -*sa* is more productive than -*mi* for deriving nouns.

Before closing this section, it is worth pointing out that for younger Japanese speakers, derived nouns with -*mi* are acceptable, especially in social networking services (SNS) such as Twitter (e.g. Uno 2015, 2017；Mogi 2018)[10]: for example, うれしみ *uresi-mi* 'the feeling of happiness' (from the adjective 嬉し（い）*uresi(i)* 'happy'), or 食べたみ *tabeta-mi* 'the state of wanting to eat' (from the desiderative form *tabe-ta(i)* 'want to eat)'. This use of -*mi* in derived nouns has been expanded in grammar and spread through the younger generation. Mogi (2018) speculates that the use of less productive or irregular -*mi* over more productive or regular -*sa* in these contexts brings about 'uniqueness' or 'freshness' in language play. He points out that by intentionally disobeying the word-formation rules, the *mi*-derived nouns have a whimsical flavour, which can be an effective way of communicating online. Yet Mogi notes that the 'deviation' from the standard word formation rules is only there on the surface. As pointed out by Sugioka (2015：79), -*mi* can add the "concrete sense" to a certain attribute of an object. For example, みかんの甘み *mikan-no ama-mi* 'tangerine's sweetness' is the concrete sense of the sweetness of a tangerine. On the other hand, -*sa* simply functions to form a noun, and thus yields more systematic meaning; thus, *mikan-no ama-sa* 'tangerine's sweetness' means the degree of a tangerine's sweetness or simply the fact that a tangerine is sweet. The observation here mirrors the fact that '-ness' in English produces a more predictable and regular meaning than '-ity' in deriv-

---

10　The verb stem *tabe* 'to eat' is affixed with the desiderative morpheme -*ta(i)* 'want', and the desiderative affix shows an adjectival conjugation.

ing nouns, which may yield irregular meaning (Embick & Marantz 2018). Given this unique property of *-mi*, Mogi (2018) concludes that the use of *-mi* among the younger generation is in fact in accord with its idiosyncratic nature.

In next section, we will look at larger linguistic units, such as phrases and sentences, and the rules regulating their formation.

4. Syntax: A Study of Phrases and Sentences

Just as words are broken down into small pieces, sentences are broken down into phrases, and phrases themselves are made of either another set of phrases or a set of words. In the same way, a word is assembled according to rules, and a phrase or a sentence is constructed in accord with specific rules. For example, 'a girl' is a noun phrase (NP), whose structure is roughly like that in (4). (See Chomsky 1957, 1970, 1981, 1993, and his subsequent work for the development of structure-building).[11]

(4)

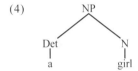

In (4), the noun 'girl' constitutes the *head* of the noun phrase, which determines the category of the entire phrase (i.e. noun) and carries the core meaning of the phrase. It is combined with the determiner 'the', forming a unit. When this NP is combined, or 'merged', with a verb, it creates a verb phrase (VP), as shown in (5).

(5)

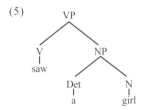

In (5), the head of the VP 'saw a girl' is the verb 'saw', which takes the

---

11　Note that the structure in (4) as well as the subsequent structures are simplified for the sake of discussion, but they are in fact more complex.

NP 'a girl' as its object. When this VP is combined with the subject NP 'Mary', a sentence (S) 'Mary saw a girl' is created, as sketched in (6).

(6)

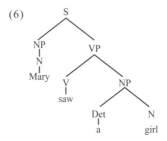

Notice that in (6), aside from S, whose notation is simplified for the sake of discussion, all the phrases have heads of the same category; that is, the subject NP has the head N 'Mary', the VP has the head V 'saw', and the object NP has the head N 'girl'. This is not a coincidence, but in fact phrase structure always shows this *endocentric*, or *headedness*, property, where a given phrase contains a head of the same category. A noun phrase without a noun, or a verb phrase without a verb, will never be formed in any language.

Let us now look at how the Japanese sentence 'Mary saw a girl' is reflected in a syntactic structure (7).

(7)

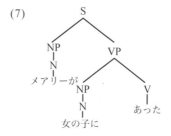

Notice that in (7), the two NPs メアリーが *Mearii*(*Mary*)-*ga* and 女の子に *onnanoko*('*girl*')-*ni* accompany case-particles -*ga* and -*ni*, respectively, which do not appear on English proper or common nouns like 'Mary' and 'girl', respectively. Case-particles illustrate a difference in the structure of Japanese and English. Another structural difference is that Japanese does not display a determiner inside the NP 女の子に , which is unlike the English equivalent 'a girl'. Further, while in English the verb appears on the left side of the phrase, with the object NP to the right, as shown in (6), in Japanese, the verb appears on the right side of the phrase, to the right of the object NP.

Similarly, the head preposition (P) of a prepositional phrase (PP) appears on the left of its associated NP in English (e.g. [PP *from Tokyo*]), and it appears on the right in Japanese (e.g. 東京に [PP *Tookyoo-ni*] 'to Tokyo'), where 東京 *Tookyoo* 'Tokyo' is an NP and に *-ni* is a P (ostposition), as shown in (8a,b). (See Baker (2001), for word order differences between English and Japanese).

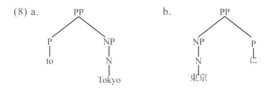

(8) a. PP — P (to) / NP — N (Tokyo)   b. PP — NP (N 東京) / P (に)

In this manner, while English and Japanese share basic properties of structure-building such as endocentricity, they are different with respect to the parameters that these properties are set to, such as the left/right position of a head and the presence or absence of case-particles and determiners.

Importantly, syntactic structure corresponds to the word order of a language: the position of a verb head in English with respect to its subject and object reflects the language's subject-verb-object (SVO) order, whereas the different positions in Japanese reflect its subject-object-verb (SOV) order. The position of heads across languages plays a very important role in capturing possible grammatical variations as well as the universality of consistent properties (like headedness) underlying languages of the world. However, this is beyond the scope of this chapter but is an important characteristic of language.

5. Conclusion

As presented throughout this chapter, language is not randomly designed but is rather systematic, following the rules of grammar. Although only a few aspects of those rules were covered in this chapter, there are rules for each component of grammar introduced in section 2: rules of phonology, morphology, syntax, and semantics. Crucially, each language follows its own rules, but at the same time shares fundamental properties with all other natural languages and obeys the basic principles of language. It should be noted that what has been covered here is very limited and is only to serve as a brief introduction to some aspects of linguistics. Thus, readers are encouraged to further study the depth and wonder of language.

References

Aronoff, Mark. 1976. *Word formation in generative grammar*. Cambridge, MA: MIT Press.

Baker, Mark. 2001. *The atoms of language*. New York: Basic Books.

Chomsky, Noam. 1957. *Syntactic structures*. The Hague: Mouton.

Chomsky, Noam. 1970. Remarks on nominalization. In Roderick. A. Jacobs & Peter S. Rosenbaum (eds.), *Readings in English transformational grammar*, 184–221. Ginn & Co.

Chomsky, Noam. 1981. *Lectures on government and binding*. Dordrecht: Foris Publication.

Chomsky, Noam. 1993. A minimalist program for linguistic theory. In Ken Hale and Samuel J. Keyser (eds.), *The view from building 20: Essays in linguistics in honor of Sylvain Bromberger*, 1–52. Cambridge, MA: The MIT Press.

Embick, Noyer & Alec Marantz. 2008. Architecture and blocking. *Linguistic Inquiry* 39. 1–53.

Kageyama, Taro. 1993. *Bunpoo to gokeisei* [Grammar and word formation]. Tokyo: Hituzi Syoboo.

Selkirk, Elisabeth O. 1982. *The syntax of words*. Cambridge, MA: The MIT Press.

Siegel, Dorothy. 1979. *Topics in English morphology*. New York: Garland.

Sugioka, Yoko. 2005. Meisika setuzi-no kinoo to imi [The function and meaning of nominalizing affixes]. In Tsuyoshi Oishi, Tetsuo Nishihara & Yoji Toyoshima (eds.), *Gendai keitairon-no tyooryuu* [The trend of modern morphology]. Tokyo: Kuroshio.

Mogi, Toshinobu. 2018. Wakamono kotoba-no "yabami" ya "uresimi" wa dokokara kiteiru mono desuka [What are the origins of the young people's words *yaba-mi* and *uresi-mi?*]. Kotoba-no gimon [Questions about language], Kotoba Kenkyuukan [Language Research Center] . National Institute for Japanese Language and Linguistics. https://kotobaken.jp/qa/yokuaru/qa-34/ (accessed on February 27, 2021).

Morita, Chigusa. 2018. A note on deadjectival nominalizations and verbalizations in Japanese. *Linguistic Research: Working Papers in English Linguistics* 28. 111–126. University of Tokyo.

Uno, Nagomi. 2015. Tuitta-ni okeru "atarasii *-mi*-kei" [The new *-mi* forms on Twitter]. *Kokubun* 123. 106–94. Ochanomizu University.

Uno, Nagomi. 2017. Tuittaa-ni miru onomatope-ni koosetu-suru setubizi *-mi* no kinoo [The function of the suffix -*mi* attached to onomatopoeia on Twitter]. *Hikaku Ninongaku Kyooiku Kenkyuu Bumon Kenkyuu Nenpoo* [Comparative Japanese Studies Annual Bulletin] 14, 183-189. Ochanomizu University.

Further Reading

O'Grady, Williams & John Archibald. 2012. *Contemporary linguistic analysis: An introduction* (*seventh edition*). Toronto: Pearson Canada.

Pinker, Steven. 1994. *The language instinct*. London: The Penguin Press.

日本語文献案内

大津由紀雄編著『はじめて学ぶ言語学：ことばの世界をさぐる 17 章』ミネルヴァ書房, 2009 年.

酒井邦嘉『言語の脳科学：脳はどのようにことばを生み出すか』中公新書, 2002 年.

三原健一・高見健一編著『日英対照 英語学の基礎』くろしお出版, 2013 年.

考えてみよう

1. 3 節で考察した, 近年の Twitter など SNS で主に使用される「つらみ」「うれしみ」等の若者語について, 通常の派生名詞である「つらさ」と「うれしさ」との比較から, どのようなニュアンスの違いが得られるのか考察してみましょう. また,「つらみ」,「うれしみ」等を文中で使用する際, どのような形態・統語的分布を見せるのかについて分析してみましょう.

2. 接辞（affix）-*ity* を伴う派生名詞には, 3 節で考察した *curiosity* の他にどのようなものがあるか調べてみましょう. また, それらの基体（base）には, どのような特徴があるかについて考えてみましょう.

3. 英語と日本語の統語的な違いには, 4 節で考察した, 格助詞・冠詞の有無, 語順の違い, の他にどのようなものがあるでしょうか. 例えば, 疑問文はこれらの言語において, それぞれどのように形成されますか. Yes/No-Question と Wh-Question はどのように形成されるでしょうか. 他にも色々な差異を考えてみましょう.

・・・・・・・・・・・・・・・・・・・・・・・・・・・・・・・・・・・・・・

杉村　美奈

Mina SUGIMURA

ことばのバリエーションと変化

Sociolinguistic Study of Language Variation: Predicting How Language Will Change

概要

　この章では，「ことばとファッションの共通点は何か」という問いに答える形で，ことばのバリエーションと変化について理解を深めます．私たちが使っていることばは，ファッションに似ています．服もことばも，それを「身につける」人の属性や場面に応じて意識的あるいは無意識的に選択され，時代とともに変化し続けるものです．ことばは，社会と密接な関わりを有し，社会的要因に応じてダイナミックに変化します．ことばの多様性とダイナミズムに目を向けることは，ことばの現在を記録・記述するだけでなく，ことばの将来を予測することにもつながります．それでは，普段何気なく使っていることばのバリエーションについて考えてみましょう．

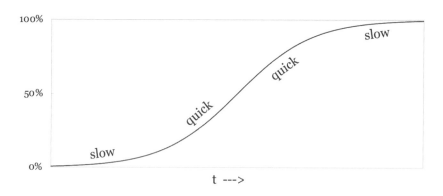

図1　緩・急・急・緩と速度を変えながら進行する言語変化のプロセス
［井上，2000「普及のSカーブ」より］

国際英語文化の中の言語変異・変化の研究

　私たちは着るものを日々選択しています．意識する・しないにかかわらず，どう見られたいか，どこに行くか，誰に会うかに応じた適切な服装選びを誰もがしています．例えば，家にいるときや友達に会うときはTシャツとジーンズのようなカジュアルな服装を選び，就職活動のための面接に行くときはダークスーツのようなフォーマルな服装を選ぶ，といった具合に，です．読者が高校生であれば，通学時には校則に従い制服を選ばざるを得ないかもしれません．しかし大学生や社会人なら，時と場合にふさわしい服装をその都度自分で選ぶことになります．自分の年齢や性別に応じて，あるいは所属集団のメンバー「らしさ」を出すことを重視して服装を決めることもあるでしょう．その結果，世の中で自分とまったく同じ服装をしている人に出会うことはほぼありません．これがファッションにおけるバリエーションです．

　同様に，ことばにもバリエーションが存在します．専門用語で「言語変異」（language variation）と言います．学校で「標準語」を学んだ多くの人は，それが唯一「正しい」ことばであると信じているかもしれません．しかし私たちは時と場合に応じて「標準語」以外にも実に多様なことばを使い分けています．しかもそれぞれの用法にはそれ相応の必然性があります．ことばの使われ方を詳しく観察すると，そこに潜む社会的な意味がはっきり見えてきます．このようにことばと社会の関係性，言い換えれば，誰が，いつ，どこで，誰に対して，どんなことばを選択しているかを紐解くことこそ，社会言語学（sociolinguistics）の最も重要な使命の1つです．

研究の楽しさ

　ことばが正誤で判断されるとの思い込みを捨てて，その運用面に目を向けてみましょう．「ら抜きことば」を例にとります．「食べられる」と「食べれる」は前者が正しく，後者の形式は一般には「誤用」と認識されています．ところが実際の会話では，実に多くの人がこの「ら抜き」形式を使っています．しかもこの「誤用」は，まったくランダムに現れるのではなく，後述する社会的要因（social factor）との関わりで生ずることもわかってきました．ならば，これはもはや「誤用」ではなく，いわゆる「標準形」とは別の社会的意味を有するれっきとした変異形なのです．変異研究と呼ばれる研究領域では，個々の言語形式がどのような社会的意味合いを有するのかを（主に数量的に）探究します．このような視点か

らことばを見たとき，正誤という尺度で判断される対象とはまったく異なる次元のことばの自然な姿が見えてきます．それは，ことばの「正しさ」は時と場合に応じて変わるということです．「正しい」ことばがただ1つしか存在しないと信じている人にとっては，変異研究はことばの再発見につながる大変興味深い分野となることでしょう．

この章のトピック

　この章では，変異研究について3つの問いを立てて考えていきます．

　1つ目は，ことばのバリエーション（変異）とは何かという問いです．「バリエーション」という用語は，一般的には「多様性」という意味で使われますが，変異研究における語義はもう少し限定的です．この分野の始祖，アメリカのウィリアム・ラバブ（William Labov, 1972）のことばを借りれば，ことばの変異とは「同じことを言うためのいくつかの形式」となります．興味深いのは，これらの言語形式が同じ意味を伝達する一方で，ことばの使い手の居住地域，出身地，社会階級，世代，性別，ことばの使用場面といった社会的要因によって好ましいとされる言語形式がしばしば異なることです．現代に見られるこのような変異を共時的変異（synchronic variation）と呼びます．この共時的変異は時代ごとに存在し，それらは少しずつ姿を変えながら過去から現代までの時間軸上でつながっています．これを，通時的変異（diachronic variation）と言います．つまり，言語変化は言語変異と切り離すことができないのです．

　2つ目は，ことばの変異は言語のどのレベルで起こるかという問いです．その答えは「言語のあらゆるレベル」です．本章では，語彙，発音，文法，綴りなどのさまざまな英語の変異の例を紹介していますが，文法変異として紹介した事例は，現代の学校文法では「誤用」とされる言語形式が実際に使用されている，または過去に「標準形」として使用されていたことを物語ります．

　3つ目は，ことばの変異という視点がなぜ必要かという問いです．変異研究が教えてくれるのは，ことばと社会の関連性です．変異を社会的要因と結びつけて考えることで，言語形式Xがどのような社会的意味を有しているかを説明できます．また，言語変化は「slow-quick-quick-slow」のS字カーブをたどり進行するという仮説があり（図1），社会的要因の1つである世代差に着目することにより将来的にことばがどう変化していくかを数量的に予測することもできます．つまり，ことばの変異に着目することは，ことばを鏡として社会を覗くことであり，ことばの将来を予測することでもあります．

研究の素材

　言語変異・変化研究分野の研究素材は，日常生活にあふれています．ふだんの言語生活で「あれ？」と思ったことが研究素材になり得ます．例えば英語の授業で「誤用」だと学んだ言語形式について「その形式を実際に誰も使っていないのか？」という批判的問いを立てれば，それはたちまち研究素材になります．筆者が行った，文頭の but の研究（Kuya, 2020b）や it is I / it is me の研究（Kuya, 2021）はそのようなきっかけから生まれました．

　また，英語の世界的拡大に関わる言語現象として，急増する外来語（カタカナ語）[1] を変異研究の枠組みで分析することも可能です．例えば英語から日本語に流入した語彙「サポート」が，「支援」や「手助け」といった既存語と同じ意味で使われる場合，これを語彙変異の問題として論じることができます．語彙の選択は一見ランダムに行われているようですが，外来語の選択と社会的要因との間に相関関係があると指摘されています（久屋，2016a；久屋，2016b）．グローバル化に伴う英語との言語接触機会の増加は，もともとあった言語の構造を大きく変容させ得る重要な要因となります．だからこそ，外来語としての英語語彙の観察は，あらゆる言語にとって重要な課題であると言えます．

　データ収集の方法はさまざまです．アンケートを利用した意識調査の分析（久屋，2016a；久屋，2016b）も可能ですが，実際に使われたことばを研究対象にすることが多いです．上述した筆者の研究（Kuya, 2020b；Kuya, 2021）で使われたデータの多くは，コーパス（corpus）と呼ばれる，話しことばや書きことばの用例を（電子的に）集めた既成の言語資料から収集されたものです．コーパスは研究者が独自につくることもできます．新聞・雑誌・書籍などの書きことばだけでなく，映画，歌，大統領の演説，インタビュー等から集めた話しことばもコーパスになり得ます．

1　外来語（カタカナ語）は通常，日本語の問題ととらえられがちです．しかし次々と流入してくる英語語彙を暫定的にカタカナで音訳しただけの語彙（短命で終わることもある）が，日本語なのか英語なのかを判断する確固たる基準はありません．話しことばではなおさら区別が困難です．その意味で，筆者は外来語を日本語と英語の中間的なもの，すなわち語彙レベルでの「コード・スイッチング」（言語の切り替え）現象の結果現れた言語形式，ととらえています．よって外来語の問題は，日本語の問題としてだけでなく，言語接触により他言語に多大な影響を与えている英語自体の問題としても扱うことができます．

研究がめざすこと

どの言語にもバリエーションは存在します．英語で言えば，イギリス英語，アメリカ英語，インド英語，フィリピン英語など世界に広がる地域的な変種（variety）が存在します．さらに，その中の1つの変種，例えばイギリス英語の中にも，さらに細かな地域変種（地域方言）や社会変種（社会方言）が存在し，時と場合に応じてさまざまな変種が使い分けられています．ことばの「正しさ」が1つではないという視点をもつことは，より高度なコミュニケーションスキルを身につけること，ひいては異文化理解力や国際感覚を育むことにもつながります．

英語を受験科目として学んできた人は，複数の正しさという視点を身につけるために「標準形」の相対化に努める必要があります．つまり，学校文法だけが常に正しいのではない，ということに気づくべきです．「標準形」はファッションで言えば，幅広い場面で使えるスーツや制服といったところでしょうか．しかし，スーツを着て自宅でくつろいだりキャンプに行ったりはしません．部屋着やキャンプウェアにもそれ相応の存在価値があるのです．同様に，「誤用」や「非標準形」とみなされていることばも，社会的意義を有している可能性は高いです．また，ことばが常に変化するという前提に立ったとき，現在の「非標準形」が将来的に「標準形」に置き換わる可能性もあります．そうした可能性を科学的に探究するとき，これまで「正しい」と信じてきたものを相対化することができます．ことばのバリエーションと変化の研究は，この相対化のプロセスそのものなのです．

Sociolinguistic Study of Language Variation: Predicting How Language Will Change

TABLE OF CONTENTS

1. Introduction: How One Dresses, How One Speaks

Every morning one awakes and makes a decision on what to wear. People choose a more appropriate item over another according to who they are, where they visit, and whom they meet. Daily casual clothes would be chosen when one is home or with one's close friends, but formal dark suits would be chosen when one has a job interview. Elements which constitute one's identity such as age, occupation, and gender would also be taken into account.

Likewise, the language one uses (or chooses) depends on who one is, whom one is talking to, what setting one is in, and so forth. The question of "who speaks what language to whom and when" (Fishman, 1965) is actually the most fundamental one for sociolinguists, who aim at describing the relationship between language and society. It is the question of how language reflects society. Observing *language variation* (or *linguistic variation*) is one of the possible concepts to answer such a question. This chapter will discuss three questions about language variation: (1) what language variation is, (2) where variation occurs, and (3) why variation matters.

2. What is Language Variation?

According to Labov, language variation refers to "many alternate ways of saying the same thing" (Labov, 1972, p. 188). The concept of language variation points out that there is more than one linguistic form to express the same thing. A detailed investigation into how people speak encourages one to discover various types of variation such as (1) *regional variation*, (2) *social variation*, and (3) *stylistic variation*.

(1) Regional variation is linguistic diversity across regions. The place where one is born and/or raised is closely related to what is called *regional dialects* or *regional varieties*. One of the most famous examples would be the contrast in vocabulary between British English and American English: e.g., "lift" vs. "elevator"; "luggage" vs. "baggage"; and "queue" vs. "line." There are many more varieties of English all over the world spoken by native/non-native speakers: Canadian English, Australian English, New Zealand English, Indian English, Jamaican English, Kenyan English, Philippine English, Singaporean English (or "Singlish"), Chinese English, Korean English, Japanese English, and so forth. Since English spoken in these regions has developed differently in many aspects, the term in the plural form—*World Englishes*—is often used to appreciate every variety of English. Furthermore, even a single variety of English, British English for instance, actually consists of more than one local variety such as Cockney (London), Scouse (Liverpool), Brummie (Birmingham), and so forth.

(2) Social variation is linguistic diversity according to the social position/ status one has. It shows that language use has a close relationship with social class, occupation, or in a broader sense, age, and gender. For example, in London, Received Pronunciation (RP for short) and Cockney are often contrasted in terms of their relation to social class. RP is traditionally regarded as *standard* for British English and is said to be more strongly associated with speakers from higher social classes. In contrast, Cockney, a dialect spoken in London, is regarded as *non-standard* and is said to be more strongly associated with speakers from lower social classes (working classes). The 1964 musical film *My Fair Lady* starring Audrey Hepburn describes the difference between RP speakers and Cockney speakers in the 1910s' London: The former pronounce [eɪ] and the latter [aɪ] in the sentence "The rain in Spain stays mainly in the plain."[2]

(3) Stylistic variation is linguistic diversity according to the setting at the time of utterance. The presence/absence of an [r] sound in New York City illustrates one of such examples. Labov (1972) reports that in New York, pronouncing [r] is considered more *prestigious* than dropping it in words like "fourth floor." The study shows that people pronounce [r] more frequently when they pay attention to their own speech. In other words, the probability of people pronouncing [r] is different according to whether the setting is formal or casual. This shows that how people use language is influenced by the formality of the social situation. The addressee also affects one's language: To one's very close friend, one can just say "Pass me the salt!" while one would try to be more polite to one's senior, superior, or a complete stranger by saying "Would you pass me the salt, please?" It is not that the one is necessarily "better" than the other in essence. One is choosing a more appropriate form for the social situation concerned (whether one is aware of it or not!).

The three above-mentioned kinds of variation, i.e., regional variation, social variation, and stylistic variation are called *synchronic* variation—linguistic diversity observed at a certain point in time. There is another type of variation, called *diachronic* variation (or *diachronic* change), which concerns linguistic diversity distributed along a timeline. As Figure 1 shows, language variation can be captured in these two dimensions.

---

2   It should be noted that the film also teaches us that, although Cockney pronunciation is often considered non-standard, it is something its speakers take pride in.

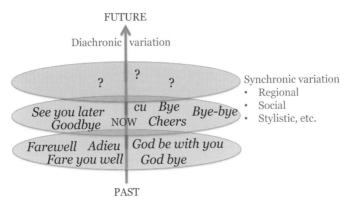

Figure 1 **The relationship between synchronic variation and diachronic variation**

Take present-day farewells, for example. One of the most popular expressions would be "goodbye" and "see you later." "Bye," "bye-bye," and "cheers" are also often used in casual settings. A more *colloquial* (casual) greeting, "cu," for instance, could appear in short digital messages. But going back to Shakespeare's time, around 1600 (at the beginning of Edo period in Japan), one might hear many people say "farewell," "fare you well," "adieu," "God bye," or "God be with you" (Crystal, 2010, p. 136). This shows that greetings used in the past are quite different from those used now and that language has changed over time. In the future, new expressions will probably replace greetings that are popular now. Of course, language change does not happen suddenly. It usually happens gradually. A few people today might still keep using "old-fashioned" greetings such as "farewell" instead of "goodbye" and "see you later." And this leads to synchronic variation. Synchronic variation, therefore, cannot be separated from diachronic variation. They are interrelated with each other.

3.　Where Does Variation Occur?

The topic of discussion now turns to the question of where language variation occurs. The answer is—at ALL levels of language. Language variation can occur at any level including *vocabulary, pronunciation, grammar, spelling,* and *meaning*. Since examples of variation in vocabulary and pronunciation have already been discussed in the explanation of regional, social and stylistic variation, attention is now paid to variation in grammar, spelling, and meaning.

Variation in grammar includes the use/non-use of *double negative* as in (1a–b), the sentence-initial use of the conjunction "but" as in (2a–b), and the usage of the first singular pronoun "I/me" after "it is" as in (3a–b), to name a few. Learners of English are usually instructed in school in the following ways: The use of double negative such as "can't + nothing" as in (1b) should be avoided as an alternative to "can't + anything" as in (1a); since the conjunction "but" should be used to combine two simple sentences as in (2a), one cannot place it at the beginning of a simple sentence as in (2b); the objective "me" (3a), not the subjective "I" (3b), is usually preferred after "it is." However, it is to be noted that the so-called "non-standard forms" like (1b) and (2b) are actually in use[3] and that there once was a time when the use of "it is I" (3b) was preferred to the present standard "it is me."[4]

(1) Grammar (double negative)
    a.   I can't eat anything.
    b.   I can't eat nothing.

                    (Trudgill, 2000, p. 35)

(2) Grammar (the sentence-initial use of the conjunction "but")
    a.   Thousands of accidents happen every day, but we all imagine that nothing will happen to us.
    b.   Thousands of accidents happen every day. But we all imagine that nothing will happen to us.

                (Adapted from Close, 1975, p. 41)

(3) Grammar (the first-person singular pronoun after "it is")
    a.   It's me! Open the door!
    b.   It's I! Open the door!

Variation in spelling can be regional. It is well known that there are several differences between British spelling and American spelling as shown in (4a–b). American spelling was established by the spelling reform movement

---

3   Kuya (2020b) shows that the use of sentence-initial "but" is on a gradual increase in written English in the past 200 years.

4   See Kuya (2021) for details of how "it is me" has replaced "it is I."

reinforced after US independence in 1776. The movement stemmed from the connection of linguistic nationalism with linguistic demands for greater correspondence of orthography with actual pronunciation (Kuya, 2020a). "Catalog" and "program" are a few of the well-known successful examples. Another example is a diachronic change in the *capitalization* of nouns. Nouns today are spelled with small letters as in (5a), but it was the fashion two or three hundred years ago to capitalize nouns as in (5b), just as German does today (Crystal, 2010, p. 135).

(4) Spelling (British vs. American)
    a. catalo<u>gu</u>e, progra<u>mm</u>e, col<u>ou</u>r, cent<u>re</u>, <u>e</u>nquiry, offen<u>ce</u> (British)
    b. catalo<u>g</u>, progra<u>m</u>, col<u>or</u>, cent<u>er</u>, <u>i</u>nquiry, offen<u>se</u> (American)

(5) Spelling (capitalization of nouns)
    a. Imitate the best <u>e</u>xamples, and have a constant <u>e</u>ye at your <u>c</u>opy.
    b. Imitate the best <u>E</u>xamples, and have a constant <u>E</u>ye at your <u>C</u>opy.
                                       (Crystal, 2010, p. 135)

Λ diachronic change in the usage of the adjective "nice" is a famous example of variation in meaning. "Nice" in the present time has a positive meaning ("good"). Many would be surprised to know that it was common for the word to convey a negative meaning ("foolish") as in (6), especially in the 14-15th centuries according to OED, *The Oxford English Dictionary* (Murray et al., 1933). This indicates that the meaning of this word has changed from negative to positive (this process is called *amelioration* in a technical terminology). A history of "silly" shows a diachronic change in meaning in the opposite direction, from positive to negative (*deterioration*). Investigation into dictionaries such as OED enables one to trace its history.

(6) Meaning
    *for-so*þ*e*[5]*, ich were* <u>*nice*</u> (13c.)
    "indeed, I was foolish"
                                            (OED, "nice")

---

5   þ *(thorn)*: a runic letter used in Old English around the 5-10th centuries, equivalent to Modern English *th*.

4. Why Does Variation Matter?

The above discussion has made it obvious that there are several types of linguistic variation and that variation can occur at all levels of language. Now, the question of why variation matters should be considered. A question arises as to what is exciting and interesting about analyzing variation. The answer is simple: Variation is NOT arbitrary. In other words, in many cases, language variation can be systematically explained by social factors, such as the speaker's age, gender, occupation, class, and the formality of the setting (as discussed above). Correlations between language use and social factors will illustrate social meaning of a specific linguistic form in a particular linguistic community. In addition, synchronic variation enables one to predict how language will change in the future since the distribution of a certain linguistic form across generations could be a reflection of *generational change* (i.e., diachronic change) (Labov, 1994, pp. 83-84).

According to a study on the distribution of vocabulary referring to "sofa" in the region of the Canada-US border in Canada, Chambers (1990) found that there existed competition between the US "couch" as opposed to the Canadian "chesterfield" (of British origin), with younger generation preferring the US form. This can be seen in Figure 2. This survey suggests the influence

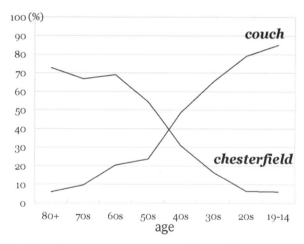

Figure 2   The distribution of the US form "couch" and the Canadian form "chesterfield" in the Canada-US border [Adapted from Chambers, 1990, p. 162]

of the speaker's age on vocabulary choice in this region. This fact tells something important about language in this region. What one can predict is that the use of the American form "couch" in this linguistic community will increase and its language will become more Americanized. This is because language usage in society usually changes in the direction toward which younger people shift. Looking at age difference in language use will enable one to predict the direction and the rate of language change. This is one of the reasons why observing the relationship between language variation and social factors is important.

5. Conclusion: Predicting How Language Will Change

As has been illustrated in the previous sections, the observation of language variation encourages one to describe dynamic aspects of a language. Both standard and non-standard (or local) varieties; formal and casual varieties; older and newer varieties have certain social meanings to the speakers. Therefore, language behavior is interpreted as social behavior showcasing the speaker's identity and their response to social needs. Language is neither uniform nor static. It is continuously changing. It would be exciting to explore more about language variation in order to predict how language will change in the future.

▌ References

Chambers, J. K. (1990). The Canada-US border as a vanishing isogloss: The evidence of *chesterfield*. *Journal of English Linguistics, 23*(1-2), 155-166.

Close, R. A. (1975). *A reference grammar for students of English*. Longman.

Crystal, D. (2010). *A little book of language*. Yale University Press.

Fishman, J. A. (1965). Who speaks what language to whom and when? *La Linguistique, 1*(2), 67-88.

Kuya, A. (2020a). A corpus analysis of the spelling reform movement in the creation of American English and Americanism (*alias* A corpus analisis of the speling riform moovment in the criasion of American English and Americanizm). *Fukuoka Jo Gakuin University Bulletin: Faculty of International Career Development* (『福岡女学院大学紀要・国際キャリア学部編』), *6,* 1-25.

Kuya, A. (2020b). Is the use of sentence-initial *but* language change in progress? *The Journal of Language in Society* (『社会言語科学』), *23*(1), 210-

225.

Kuya, A. (2021). A corpus-based variationist approach to the use of *it is I* and *it is me* in COHA: A real-time observation of a syntactic change nearing completion. *Gengo Kenkyu*（『言語研究』）, *159*, 7-35.

Labov, W. (1972). *Sociolinguistic patterns*. Basil Blackwell.

Labov, W. (1994). *Principles of linguistic change, Vol. 1: Internal factors*. Blackwell.

Murray, J. A. H. et al. (1933). *The Oxford English dictionary* (Being a corrected re-issue with an introduction, supplement, and bibliography of *A new English dictionary on historical principles*), *Vol. VII: N-Poy*. Clarendon Press.

Trudgill, P. (2000). *Sociolinguistics: An introduction to language and society* (Fourth edition). Penguin Books.

井上史雄（2000）『東北方言の変遷：庄内方言歴史言語学的貢献』秋山書店.

久屋愛実（2016a）「見かけ上の時間を利用した外来語使用意識の通時変化予測」『日本語の研究』12,（4）, 69-85.

久屋愛実（2016b）「外来語使用に係るスタイルの制約：「サポート」と既存語との使い分けにみる話者内バリエーション」『社会言語科学』19,（1）, 190-206.

Further Reading

Kuya, A. (2019). *The diffusion of Western loanwords in contemporary Japanese: A variationist approach* (Hituzi Linguistics in English 30). Hituzi Syobo.

Meyerhoff, M. (2006). *Introducing sociolinguistics*. Routledge.

日本語文献案内

中尾俊夫他『社会言語学概論：日本語と英語の例で学ぶ社会言語学』くろしお出版, 1997 年.

日比谷潤子編著『はじめて学ぶ社会言語学：ことばのバリエーションを考える 14 章』ミネルヴァ書房, 2012 年.

考えてみよう

1. 等位接続詞の but が文頭に出現する用例を新聞・雑誌・ブログ記事などから探してみましょう. 最も頻出する媒体はどれでしょうか（手始めに, 本文

中から文頭の but を探してみましょう).

2. 形容詞 silly の意味の変遷を OED (*Oxford English Dictionary*)[6] で調べて
   みましょう.

3. 英語の世界的な拡大は，日本語に語彙バリエーションをもたらしました．例
   えば，「サポート／支援」「メリケン粉／小麦粉」「ハンガー／衣紋掛け」「ター
   トルネック／とっくり」といった英語由来の語彙（「カタカナ語」）と既存語
   （和語・漢語）の使用に，地域的（regional）・社会的（social）・文体的
   （stylistic）な分布差が見られるか調べてみましょう[7].

4. 芸能人が標準語（standard variety）と方言（local variety）を番組によっ
   て使い分けている例を探してみましょう．なぜそのような切り替えを行うの
   か，考察しましょう.

・・

久屋　愛実
Aimi KUYA

6　オンラインバージョンもある．OED Online［https://www.oed.com/］
7　日本語における英語由来の語彙（「カタカナ語」）と既存語（和語・漢語）の語彙バリエーショ
　ン（lexical variation）の問題は久屋（2016a, 2016b），Kuya（2019）に詳しい（Further
　Reading を参照）.

社会文化的視座による異文化インターアクションと第二言語習得

Sociocultural Perspectives on Intercultural Interactions and Second Language Acquisition

概要

　本章では，日々の暮らしの中で，人々がことばをどのように使い，またどのように習得するかを社会・文化との関連性から考察します．ことばそのものや脳内の言語処理に着目する伝統的な研究分野と異なるこの手法は，「ポスト構造主義」と呼ばれ，さまざまな社会文化理論を生み出してきました．言語行動は社会的で，常に一定ではなく状況によって異なり，経時的に変化するものです．社会文化理論は言語学習者・使用者を取り巻く環境に着目しながら言語行動プロセスを明らかにすることを目的としています．特に本章では，異文化インターアクション（後述）と第二言語習得に焦点を当て，4つの異なる観点（異文化適応，アイデンティティ，相互文化的能力，言語景観）から社会文化的アプローチを考察します．なお，会話であれ文書でのやり取りであれ，意思の疎通は人と人との関係性の上に成り立つ相互行為（インターアクション）であることを重視し，本章では，異文化コミュニケーションではなく「異文化インターアクション」という表現を用います．

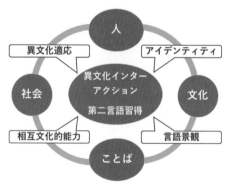

図1　社会文化的視座の概念図

国際英語文化と応用言語学研究

　社会のグローバル化が進む中，複数の文化規範，慣習が混在するようになり，異文化接触の機会が増加してきました．これに伴い，応用言語学では，人とことばを社会的，文化的につなぎ合わせる社会文化的視座の重要性が一層高まってきています．どのような経緯で異文化接触が起こるのでしょうか．また，私たちは異文化接触にどう対処すべきなのでしょうか．文化を過剰に一般化することを回避し，文化的ステレオタイプを払拭するためには，異文化接触に起因する相互行為を紐解くことが大切です．その際に，表に現れる言語行動だけではなく，背後に隠れた「言語に対する行動（behavior toward language）」（Fishman, 1972）に着目し，人々が文化的相違点・類似点を留意，評価し，相互行為を調整していく一連のプロセスを分析すると効果的です．さらに，人々が「どこで」「誰と」「どのような目的で」「どのような立場で」「何を」もとに対話するのかをさまざまな社会文化的要因と照らし合わせながら考察することも必要となります．

研究の大切さ

　この分野の研究は，話しことば・書きことばだけではなく，ことばの使い手として「人」を深く分析し，社会的な活動を通して人々のことばの営みを探るという意義をもっています．そのため，いろいろな方々からさまざまな話を伺う楽しさがあります．インタビューでは，研究者はよき聞き手となり，研究対象者に自らの言語使用を客観的に振り返る機会を与え，新たな学びへと繋がる内省のきっかけを提供するという役割も兼ねています．また，一般化されている事象を批判的に考察し，時には例外の重要性を見出すことで，物事のとらえ方の多様性を受け入れ，客観的な文化意識を高めることができます．このような研究に取り組むことで，表面的な物事の解釈に留まることなく，常に深く物事を考える姿勢を養うことができることも魅力の１つです．

この章のトピック

異文化適応
　まずは代表的な社会文化理論の１つである「言語の社会化（language socialization）」（Duff, 2010）を用いて異文化適応における第二言語習得を考

えてみましょう．留学や移民などで第二言語学習者が新たな異文化コミュニティに参加し，第二言語を習得していくには，その言語を巧みに操る人々とのさまざまな相互行為が必要となります（Duff, 2010）．また，主な所属先となるコミュニティの他にもさまざまな公的・私的コミュニティやネットワークを通して異文化適応が促進されます．例えば，海外留学の場合は，同じ国や他の国から来た留学生，同じ民族的背景をもつ学生，同じ趣味をもつ学生などと私的コミュニティ・ネットワークを形成することができます．これらも異文化に慣れ親しむための協働の輪となり，第二言語能力を高めていく場となり得るのです．英語本文Example 1 の中国系インドネシア人留学生エリックさんは，民族性を最大限に活用して自らの居場所を確保し，主体的に参加できるコミュニティをつくり上げました．この事例では，特定コミュニティへの社会化が，留学生活を円滑に進めていく基盤となり，自らに合った第二言語習得の術を見出す重要な要因となることが例証されています．

アイデンティティ

　社会文化的視座はことばとアイデンティティの研究にも影響を与えています．アイデンティティと言えば，国籍，民族，宗教などに基づくマクロなものとしてとらえられがちですが，自己認識が変化することで形成されるミクロなアイデンティティも存在します．これらはポスト構造主義的アイデンティティ（poststructuralist identity）や状況に埋め込まれたアイデンティティ（situated identity）と呼ばれ，時空間によって変化し，言語学習や言語使用に影響を与えると考えられています．Example 2 はポーランド語訛りの英語とオーストラリア英語を家庭内外で使い分けていたポーランド系オーストラリア人のアリーナさんの事例です．アリーナさんは留学を機に英語話者としての自己を客観的に見直すとともに自分に合った英語の話し方を見出し，ポーランド語訛りの英語話者としてのアイデンティティを強めていきました．

　このポスト構造主義的アイデンティティから派生し，さらに具体化された概念が，「投資（investment）」（Norton, 2010）です．この「投資」の概念は，もともと心理学寄りであった第二言語学習モチベーション理論に社会文化的要素を加え，学習意欲に基づく実際の行動に焦点を当てています．行動を起こす際の状況性や他者との関連性を考慮し，目標達成のためにどのように労力を割き，何をするのかに着目した概念です．この「投資」を別の理論的概念「資本（capital）」（Bourdieu, 1986）と組み合わせていくと効果的です．ここでの「資本」は「投資」の結果として言語学習者・使用者が得る知識，スキル，人脈などを指します．

　Darvin と Norton（2015）の研究では，カナダに住む 16 歳のフィリピン人学生の事例が紹介されています．この学生は，英語でのオンライン為替取引講座

に年齢を伏せて積極的に参加し，他の参加者との交流に自らの労力を「投資」し，起業家向けの英語知識と為替取引学習者同士の英語人脈を「資本」として構築しました．この「投資」により，起業家の卵としての第二言語アイデンティティを高めていったのです．

相互文化的能力

　相互文化的能力（intercultural competence）もポスト構造主義の影響を強く受け，社会文化的発達を遂げてきた理論と言えるでしょう．この理論は，文法能力，社会言語能力，社会文化能力などから成るコミュニケーション能力に，異文化の接触性を加えたもので，Byram（2008）や Deardorff（2006）がその形成要素となるいくつかの基準を提唱しています．Example 3 はオーストラリアの大学でテニスのチーム練習を始めようとしている日本人留学生 1 名，オーストラリア人学生 1 名，マレーシア人留学生 2 名の会話で，日本人留学生の発言により場が凍りついてしまった事例です．この事例の日本人留学生は，相互文化的能力を形成する敬意，寛容さ，好奇心はある程度伴っているものの，差別的な表現に関する理解や社会文化的な知識のなどの他の要素が十分ではなく，相互文化的能力が発達途中であることがわかります．この事例では，相互文化的能力が不十分な場合，社交性を高めようとする積極的な発言が意に反して逆効果となりうることが例示されています．

言語景観

　多文化主義の研究から発展した言語景観研究もことばと私たちの日々の営みを社会文化的視座から考察するには有効です．この分野では，もともとは，公共の標識，広告，店の看板などが対象でしたが，テクノロジーの進化に伴いその範囲

図 2　比較対象として **Sushi** が用いられた英語景観（**Less Carbs Than A Sushi Roll**）：巻き寿司よりも炭水化物が少ないことを強調するハンバーガー店のポスター［メルボルン，2016年筆者撮影］

も拡大してきており，現在では書きことばだけではなく，イメージ，音，図，落書き，タトゥー，匂い，人々などが総合的に言語景観をつくり出すと考えられています（Shohamy, 2019）．このような観点から，つくり手が標識や看板を通して何を伝えたいのか，読み手がどのようにそれらを解釈するか，構成やレイアウトがその解釈にどの程度影響を与えるかなどを調査し，人々，標識，空間，時間の相互作用を明らかにするのがこの研究分野の特徴です（Gorter, 2013）．特に，多言語標識を人々の営み，アイデンティティ，相互文化的能力，言語教育などと組み合わせて考察してみると面白い発見を得ることができるでしょう．

研究の素材

　実際の会話や文章の分析もしますが，言語学習者・使用者へのアンケートやインタビューで得たデータが中心となります．主に，大量のサンプルをもとに統計を用いて研究結果を数字で表す量的研究と研究対象者の具体的な回答を分析する質的研究に分かれますが，言語に対する行動を聞き出し，人々のことばの営みを深く探っていく上では，質的な考察が適していると言えます．

研究がめざすこと

　SNS，ビデオチャットなどを含むオンラインツールを通してインターアクションの形態が多様化する昨今，異文化接触の概念そのものを再考する必要性が高まってきています．異文化インターアクション研究や第二言語習得研究に社会文化的視座を適用することで，ことばそのものの研究だけでは見えてこない，異文化接触に起因する言語行動とその背後にある社会文化的，認知的要因の探究をめざします．このようなミクロな取り組みが，新たな社会言語学的洞察を得る足がかりになると期待されます．また，日々の生活の中で新種の異文化接触がなぜ，どのように発生し，ことばの営みにどのような影響を及ぼすのかを明らかにすることも当該分野のこれからの目標となるでしょう．これにより，グローバル化時代の異文化接触との向き合い方やそれに伴うアイデンティティ形成をより深く考察することが可能になると考えられます．

Sociocultural Perspectives on Intercultural Interactions and Second Language Acquisition

TABLE OF CONTENTS

1. Introduction

The study of language began with the analysis of language itself, including grammar and text structures, and then expanded to investigate language processing in the brain, which focuses on the human ability to acquire grammatical patterns. These two major approaches are regarded as traditional research paradigms in the field of linguistics. While the importance of these paradigms has been appreciated by many linguists, a number of researchers have suggested that the social and cultural aspects of language learning and use should be considered along with analyses of textual structures and mental processes. As a result, poststructuralist theories of language, which are also known as sociocultural theories, have emerged (cf. Norton, 2010). This perspective stresses that discourse—language use in or as a result of communicative acts—is produced by what we usually do in daily life, and that discourse contributes to reproducing our daily activities as well. These theories also see language behavior as not static but dynamic, since it frequently changes with social and cultural influences.

Thus, the poststructuralist view, which focuses on how discourse differs depending on different social situations in daily life, has enabled us not only to examine the text itself, but also to analyze the processes in which people learn and/or use language in relation to social environments. These processes include "behavior toward language" in which people consider how to use and adjust language to interact with others properly and effectively (Fishman, 1972). It is therefore necessary to explore further why and how behavior toward language as well as language behavior occurs, taking into account the sociocultural factors affecting discourse. These factors include:

(1) social contexts where we use language
(2) people with whom we interact
(3) the topics that we talk about
(4) the roles we play in a target community

We can investigate these sociocultural factors more comprehensively by analyzing them in relation to cognitive factors. By considering the cognitive aspects of language users and/or learners, we not only investigate their knowledge, beliefs, and attitudes toward the target discourse, but also explore how they perceive such sociocultural factors and evaluate their own language learning and use. Integrating cognitive factors into sociocultural analysis thus encourages us to discuss language behavior and behavior toward language from inside and outside the human mind.

Along with this movement, such sociocultural perspectives have been applied in the research areas of intercultural interactions and second language acquisition (SLA). In an era of globalization, the importance of sociocultural approaches has further increased, because we have had more opportunities to encounter cultural contact, which involves conflicts between two or more different cultural norms and practices. In considering why and how cultural contact occurs, and how to deal with such contact, we need to gain a deeper understanding of how intercultural interactions and second language (L2) learning are "situated" and socially "co-constructed." Recently, both "situated" and "co-constructed" have become important keywords in applied linguistics, because language learning and use are situationally different and take place in relation to others. Taking into account these two components, the following sections of this chapter will illustrate several sociocultural theories to explain intercultural interactions and SLA in more detail.

2. Intercultural Adjustment and Identity
Adjustment to Study Abroad Contexts

The first sociocultural theory is *language socialization* (Duff, 2010), which emphasizes the process of learning through activities in a specific community. This theory has been actively used to investigate how international students adjust to study abroad contexts. In explaining language socialization, Duff (2010) claimed that L2 learners would effectively learn L2 through interactions with others who are more proficient in the target language, when they participate in a community as novice members. However, we should not ignore that language socialization could be a little broad and ambitious as a concept, because not all novice members become fuller participants through their participation in a specific community. It is also important to note that the host community to which they belong may not necessarily be the one to which they feel the need to adjust. Kramsch's (1993) notion of a *third place* indicates that apart from their home and host communities, L2 learners might find another place between their first and second cultures to position themselves favorably, such as communities of study abroad students, people of the same nationality or the same ethnic background, people with the same hobbies, and so on. Please look at Eric's case in Example 1.

Example 1

A Chinese Indonesian postgraduate student who majored in Information Technology at an Australian university, Eric, developed his third place with other international classmates from Southeast Asia through his study. His third place enabled him to feel comfortable interacting with others in Southeast Asian English. These networks helped him improve his academic knowledge and skills as well. By having this third place, Eric regarded Malaysian and Singaporean students in his course as role models, rather than Australian students, and learned Southeast Asian English as the main tool of interaction in Australia. Eric successfully obtained a master's degree and has been working at an ethnic Chinese company in Australia.

Eric made the most of his ethnicity to establish a place that brought him success in his academic life. His case suggests that having a third place where students comfortably participate can facilitate their academic achievement while studying abroad.

A frequently changing sense of self

The *poststructuralist identity* is the other sociocultural approach which enables us to view intercultural interactions and SLA (Norton, 2010). Speaking of identity, we tend to imagine the ones based on ethnicity, nationality, and religion, which no one can deny as a part of one's demographic background. However, in contrast to macro-level identities, language users and/or learners form a sense of self—a micro-level identity—which is subject to change depending on the situation. This is also called a *situated identity*. Focusing on power relations with others and their relationship to social environments, Norton (2010) claimed that people tend to have multiple identities across time and space, and that such identities affect their language learning and use. Example 2 is the case of a Polish Australian woman, Alina, who changed her first language (L1) identity by using Australian English and Polish English differently depending on the situation.

Example 2

Alina was the daughter of Polish immigrants, born and brought up in Australia. When she talked to her family at home, she spoke Polish or Polish-accented English, with her strong awareness of her Polish background. On the other hand, Alina deliberately used Australian English to communicate with her school friends, because she knew that she might be excluded if she used accented English. However, during her one-academic-year study in Japan in Year 11 (the second year of senior high school), she noticed that there were a variety of "Englishes." As she saw some Japanese people speaking English using the Japanese pronunciation system, she realized that she did not always have to speak like her Australian friends. As she positively accepted the ways they unwittingly reflected their ethnicity in their English, she gradually preferred her own Polish English, through which she was able to better express her feelings. Particularly, Alina realized that the soft and flat intonation of Polish English suited her personality more. After returning to Australia, she totally switched to Polish English in every situation.

By reviewing how Japanese people speak English as a foreign language, Alina evaluated her own English use and transformed her L1 identity. In this way, she found her own way of speaking English and how to be herself in a multicultural society. After graduating from senior high school, she started studying law, specializing in migration law to help ethnic minorities in Australia in the future.

Furthermore, people who have a unique connection to Japan and Australia are reported on one of the subpages of the website, "Language on the Move" organized by Ingrid Piller. Among the individually different experiences, the case of Mayu Kondo, who works as a hospital scientist in Australia, indicates that her situated identities have been changing over time. Her identity development started as a Japanese learner of English at an English language school in Australia. During her subsequent study of hospitality management at a vocational school, she identified herself as not an ESL (English as a second language) learner, but as an ESL user who used English as a means of interaction in her social and academic life. Throughout her further study of nutrition at university, her identity was expanded to include her L2 academic self, where she regarded herself as an ESL international student, but also as the same full-time university student as local Australians. Her case indicates that by having this type of identity, she felt the need to compete with these local students while envisaging her future career in Australia. Now, as a hospital scientist, she gained her professional identity in L2 by making the most of her qualifications. Kondo has also developed her L2 identity as a member of a multicultural society in Australia. As discussed in these two cases, it is important to analyze the processes of identity transformations. In doing so, we can see that identity is a site of struggle and changing over time (Norton, 2010).

Investment and Capital

The poststructuralist identity has been further elaborated by the concept of *investment* (Norton, 2010). Here, Norton added sociocultural aspects of language learning to the psychologically oriented approach to L2 learning motivation, focusing on learners' changing identities and what they do while balancing power relations with others. Norton pointed out that even though they are motivated to learn, such motivation is not always followed by specific actions, depending on the context. The concept thus enables us to explore how learners allocate efforts and invest in achieving their learning goals, as well as how motivated they are. The other concept related to investment is *capital*, which represents knowledge and skills language users and/or learners gain as a result of investment (Bourdieu, 1986). While both investment and capital sound like economic terms, they have been used along with L2 identity in the field of applied linguistics. In particular, Darvin and Norton (2015) have suggested that investment should be considered in relation to capital, identity, and ideology (see Figure 1). For example, their study of digital literacy illustrated the relationship between investment and these three components, focusing on a 16-year-old Filipino participant in Canada, Ayrton. Modeling his father's suc-

Figure 1   Darvin and Norton's 2015 Model of Investment

cess as an entrepreneur, Ayrton participated in an online currency trading course. Modifying his social media profile and concealing his age, he actively discussed market trends with professionals online in English. Through such investment, he gained capital in the forms of entrepreneurial knowledge and global networks of other currency trading learners. This capital enabled him to develop his strong entrepreneurial identity and ideology in L2.

Focusing on *individual networks of practice* (INoP), Zappa-Hollman and Duff's (2015) study revealed Mexican students' investments in a Canadian university. INoP is a concept expanded from *community of practice* (CoP) (Lave & Wenger, 1991). In applied linguistics, CoP represents the community where novice members practice L2 in various social situations in multiple ways to be fuller participants (cf. Lave & Wenger, 1991). However, some researchers have claimed that it is important to consider opportunities for learning not only in a specific community, but also through various others (Duff & Talmy, 2011). By emphasizing individual networks, the newly emerged concept of INoP enables us to analyze individuals' personal relationships within or beyond a community (Zappa-Hollman & Duff, 2015). One of the participants in Zappa-Hollman and Duff's study, Raquel, developed INoPs with students from different cultures. The strongest INoP she invested in was with an Australian woman, Stephanie, who had just finished her degree. The slang, colloquial expressions, and pronunciations that Stephanie taught her helped Raquel improve her spoken English. Stephanie also provided editing support to Raquel by pointing out written English mistakes in her politics course assignments. Zappa-Hollman and Duff's study indicated that international students can grow a strong sense of agency during study abroad by drawing on a wide range of resources, and utilizing many forms of capital.

3. Intercultural Competence

The poststructuralist view has also contributed to the sociocultural development of *intercultural competence*. Based on the original model of *communicative competence* defined by Hymes (1972), neo-Hymesian models have emerged, specifying grammatical, discourse, sociolinguistic, strategic, sociocultural competence, and so on (cf. Canale & Swain, 1980; Neustupný, 1985). These models emphasize that grammatical knowledge and skills do not suffice in L2 interactions; rather, we need to understand how language should be used in social contexts, considering how to use situationally different expressions and how to perform based on sociocultural knowledge.

Intercultural competence is a theory that has been expanded from neo-Hymesian models. Given that several researchers have defined such competence in different ways, this chapter introduces Byram's (2008) *intercultural communicative competence* (ICC), and Deardorff's (2006) *intercultural competence*. Byram suggested five criteria for ICC. Among the five criteria, "attitudes" toward one's own and other cultures and "knowledge" of norms and practices in one's own and other countries are categorized as a foundation for ICC. Based on these two criteria, "skills of interpreting and relating" and "skills of discovery and interaction" can be developed. The former refers to the ability to explain and judge the characteristics of one's own and other cultures and relate them to each other. The latter refers to the ability to gain new cultural knowledge and interact well with others. According to Byram, through these skills, people can obtain "critical cultural awareness," whereby one evaluates what people usually do in one's own and other cultures from a neutral position. The previously shown Mayu Kondo's case also reveals her development of ICC. Regarding how to get along with others in her culturally diverse workplace, she emphasized the following points in an interview:

(1) "You can't read other people's mind."
(2) "No such thing as common sense"

As indicated in these comments, she understands her status as a cultural outsider, and considers how to interact with others by interpreting coworkers' opinions favorably and relating them to her way of thinking. In doing so, it seems that she has developed critical cultural awareness while evaluating the individually different views in her multicultural workplace neutrally.

Similarly, Deardorff (2006) stressed the process of intercultural competence more explicitly by defining the *pyramid* and *process* models. These models specified four different stages, including "requisite attitudes," "knowledge and comprehension," "desired internal outcome," and "desired external outcome."

Example 3 below is a dialog between a Japanese female student (JS), an Australian female student (AS), and two Malaysian female students (MSs) at a university tennis center in Australia. For their team practice, they discussed which court they should play on.

Example 3
AS: The sun's out now. I wanna have a hit under the sun.
JS: No, let's play in the shade. I'm jealous of your white skin. I want to be like you.
MSs: ...
AS: ...

The dialog shows that the Japanese student's insufficient intercultural competence did not produce a desired external outcome, because it caused the others to feel at a loss as to how to respond to her comment. Indeed, she meant no harm, and adopted a friendly attitude toward her Australian friend with respect, openness, and curiosity. However, her sociocultural knowledge, sociolinguistic awareness, and understanding of politically correct expressions, were insufficient. She did not even seem to realize that one's complexion is a sensitive topic of discussion.

4. Linguistic Landscape

The sociocultural perspectives of language use are also reflected in the *linguistic landscape* (LL). Expanding from research on multiculturalism, LL is a theory developed relatively recently in sociolinguistics. LL enables us to investigate displayed language in public spaces, and consider the mutual relationships among language, culture, and language users. Landry and Bourhis (1997) defined LL as shaped by the language of public signs, advertising billboards, shop signs in a particular space, such as a territory, town, street, and region. Shohamy (2019) claimed that this classic definition has been expanded by the emergence of the internet and other technological devices. LL can also be regarded as involving any display in public spaces, because written texts have increasingly been combined with "images, sounds, drawings, movements, visuals, graffiti, tattoos, colors, smells, and people" (Shohamy, 2019, p. 27). From this perspective, LL research is designed to reveal the interactions among people, signage, space, and time by exploring what signage producers intend to deliver, how readers interpret signage, and how devices and layouts influence their interpretations of signage (Gorter, 2013).

Based on these definitions, several researchers have investigated the LL in Japan. Backhaus (2006) undertook quantitative research on LL in Tokyo, focusing on official and non-official bilingual signs. Considering that quantitative LL research has not investigated how people interpret multilingual signs sufficiently, Rowland (2016) conducted a qualitative study to explore Japanese students' perceptions of such signs. Barrs (2015) analyzed errors in the use of English in relation to English loanwords in the Japanese LL, focusing on the phonological and orthographic differences between Japanese and English. LL has furthermore been investigated as a tool for language teaching and learning. By investigating an LL project conducted by undergraduate linguistics students in Australia, Hatoss (2019) found that LL can serve as a pedagogical tool to improve students' intercultural competence.

As Shohamy (2019, p. 32) claims, LL is "a tip of the iceberg that leads to deeper cultural and social interpretations of societal issues." Thus, research on LL provides us with useful markers to delve deeper into diversified modes of intercultural interactions and to reconsider various relationships between culture, society, and language more comprehensively.

5. Conclusion

Sociocultural approaches to intercultural interactions and SLA enable us to consider human actions through language use, behavior toward language, and how to deal with cultural contact from different angles. Different people in different situations construct different interaction styles, and different micro identities in relation to others. Viewing discourse as situated and socially co-constructed, it is crucial to analyze who interacts with whom, in what context, and for what purpose. A mere analysis of text does not lead us to comprehensively understand interactions, cultural contact, and SLA. By examining why and/or how linguistic phenomena happen, we should explore the sociocultural and cognitive factors behind communicative acts.

Given the growing sociolinguistic awareness of languages as mobile resources in a globalized world (Blommaert, 2010), we can see that cultural contact not only involves conflicts, but also causes positive linguistic phenomena. In particular, cultural contact can be a site of struggle that provides people with opportunities to develop situated identities, capital, and intercultural competence in the process of L2 socialization. Due to the rise of multimodality, including SNS, video chats, and other online tools, there currently exist various types of cultural contact. Hence, the concept of cultural contact itself needs to be re-explored to discover why and how new types of contact occur and how they affect language learning and use. By investigating these issues, we stand to gain more sociocultural insight into intercultural interactions and SLA, and would facilitate the processes through which L2 learners develop a sense of L2 self and improve their intercultural competence.

References

Backhaus, P. (2006). Multilingualism in Tokyo: A look into the linguistic landscape. *International Journal of Multilingualism, 3* (1), 52-66.

Barrs, K. (2015). Errors in the use of English in the Japanese linguistic landscape. *English Today 124, 31* (4), 30-33.

Blommaert, J. (2010). *The sociolinguistics of globalization*. Cambridge University Press.

Bourdieu, P. (1986). The forms of capital. In J. F. Richardson (Ed.), *Handbook of theory and research for the sociology of education* (pp. 241-258). Greenwood Press.

Byram, M. (2008). *From foreign language education to education for intercultural citizenship: Essays and reflections*. Multilingual Matters.

Canale, M., & Swain, M. (1980). Theoretical bases of communicative approaches to second language teaching and testing. *Applied Linguistics, I* (1), 1-47.

Darvin, R., & Norton, B. (2015). Identity and a model of investment in applied linguistics. *Annual Review of Applied Linguistics, 35,* 36-56.

Deardorff, D. K. (2006). Identification and assessment of intercultural competence as a student outcome of internationalization. *Journal Studies in International Education, 10* (3), 241-266.

Duff, P. A. (2010). Language socialization into academic discourse communities. *Annual Review of Applied Linguistics, 30*, 169-192.

Duff, P. A., & Talmy, S. (2011). Language socialization approaches to second language acquisition: Social, cultural, and linguistic development in additional languages. In D. Atkinson (Ed.), *Alternative approaches to second language acquisition* (pp. 95-116). Routledge.

Fishman, J. A. (1972). *The sociology of language: An interdisciplinary social science approach to language in society*. Newbury House Publishers.

Gorter, D. (2013). Linguistic landscapes in a multilingual world. *Annual Review of Applied Linguistics, 33*, 190-212.

Hatoss, A. (2019). Linguistic landscapes: An experiential learning project for developing intercultural competence. *Australian Review of Applied Linguistics, 42*(2), 146-170.

Hymes, D. H. (1972). On communicative competence. In J. B. Pride & J. Holmes (Eds.), *Sociolinguistics* (pp. 269-293). Penguin Books.

Kramsch, C. (1993). *Context and culture in language teaching*. Oxford University Press.

Landry, R., & Bourhis, R. Y. (1997). Linguistic landscape and ethnolinguistic vitality: An empirical study. *Journal of Language and Social Psychology, 16* (1), 23-49.

Lave, J., & Wenger, E. (1991). *Situated learning: Legitimate peripheral participation*. Cambridge University Press.

Neustupný, J. V. (1985). Problems in Australian-Japanese contact situations. In J. B. Pride (Ed.), *Cross-cultural encounters: Communication and miscommunication* (pp. 44-63). River Seine.

Norton, B. (2010). Language and identity. In N. H. Hornberger & S. L. McKay (Eds.), *Sociolinguistics and language education* (pp. 349-369). Multilingual Matters.

Piller, I. (n.d.) *Japanese on the move*. Language on the move. https://www.languageonthemove.com/japanese-on-the-move

Rowland, L. (2016). English in the Japanese linguistic landscape: A motive analysis. *Journal of Multilingual and Multicultural Development, 37*(1), 40-55.

Shohamy, E. (2019). Linguistic landscape after a decade: An overview of themes, debates and future directions. In M. Pütz & N. Mundt (Eds.), *Expanding the linguistic landscape: Linguistic diversity, multimodality and the use of space as a semiotic resource* (pp. 25-37). Multilingual Matters.

Zappa-Hollman, S., & Duff, P. A. (2015). Academic English socialization through individual networks of practice. *TESOL Quarterly, 49*(2), 333-368.

Further Reading

Kanno, Y. (2003). *Negotiating bilingual and bicultural identities: Japanese returnees betwixt two worlds*. Routledge.

Morita, N. (2004). Negotiating participation and identity in second language academic communities. *TESOL Quarterly, 38*, 573-603.

日本語文献案内

東照二『社会言語学入門:生きた言葉のおもしろさに迫る』改訂版,研究社,2009年.
根本浩行「第二言語習得における社会文化的アプローチ」『金沢大学言語文化論叢』16, 2012, 19-38.

考えてみよう

1. 出身地が異なる友達とコミュニケーションをとる上で違和感を覚えたことはありませんか? どのような違和感か, どうして違和感が生じたか, 考えてみましょう.

2. 場面によることばの使い分けを考えてみましょう. 大学, 家庭, アルバイト先, 部活・サークルなどの場面でことばの使い方はどのように変わりますか? また, これらの場面でアイデンティティはどのように変化しているでしょうか? 「どのような立場で」,「誰と」,「どのような状況で」,「どのような目的で」コミュニケーションをとるかを考察して, アイデンティティの変化を分析してみましょう.

3. 身の回りもしくはメディア上の英語標識・スローガン (部分的な英語の使用も含む) を集めて, どのような目的で英語が使用されているか考えてみましょう.

・・

根本　浩行
Hiroyuki NEMOTO

バイリンガル教育の視点から見た
日本の英語教育

Teaching English in Japan with a
Bilingual Education Perspective

概要

　皆さんは「バイリンガル教育研究」と聞くと，どのような学問領域を想像するでしょうか．バイリンガルになるための教育，つまり外国語教授法研究の一種だと思うかもしれません．ところが，外国語教授法研究はバイリンガル教育研究のほんの一部でしかありません．実際，バイリンガル教育研究は，人として生きる上での領域の多くに関係があります．つまり，教育とは何か，言語とは何か，言語を学ぶとはどういうことかを考え，さらに，バイリンガルであることは個人のアイデンティティとどう関わるのか，そして多言語社会の実際と理想とは何なのかを考える学際的な研究領域なのです．この章では，バイリンガル教育研究の主要な理論を概観し，バイリンガル教育研究が扱うさまざまな領域を見た後，こうした研究が日本の英語教育に与える示唆について考えます．その中で特に重要となるのは，「モノリンガル的なバイリンガルのとらえ方」と「バイリンガル的なバイリンガルのとらえ方」の対比です．

　図1，2はバイリンガルの頭の中がどのようになっているのか模式的に表したものです．一般的には多くの人が左側の SUP モデルのようなイメージをもっているのではないでしょうか．「A さんは英語が上手になったから，日本語が少し変になってきたね」というような言説はこのような理解，つまり「モノリンガル的なバイリンガルのとらえ方」に基づいています．1 つの言語の部屋が大きくなるともう一方の言語の部屋が縮んでしまう，というイメージでしょう．しかし，バイリンガル教育研究の理論では，バイリンガルの頭の中を右側の CUP モデルのようにイメージします．バイリンガルのもつ言語資源は別々の部屋に分かれて置いてあるのではなく，一体として混在していて，必要に応じてそれぞれの言語で考えを取り出すことができる，というイメージです．

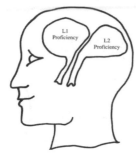

図1　The Separate Underlying Proficiency (SUP) model of bilingualism[Cummins, 1980/2001, p. 131]

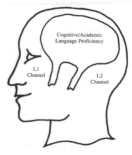

図2　The Common Underlying Proficiency (CUP) model of bilingualism[Cummins, 1980/2001, p. 132]

国際英語文化の中のバイリンガル教育研究

　ネィティブスピーカーに拙い英語で話しかけてわかってもらえなかったときに，「困った」ではなく「申し訳ない」「恥ずかしい」と思ったことはありませんか．でもよく考えてみると，悪いことをしたわけではないのに，なぜ「申し訳ない」気持ちになるのでしょうか．自分にとって母語ではない言葉をうまく話せないことが，なぜ「恥ずかしい」ことになるのでしょうか．

　こうした感情の背後には，英語の重要性を無批判に受け入れ，ネィティブスピーカーの話し方を規範とする見方が存在していることが考えられます．第二言語習得研究では目標言語の運用能力のみを評価基準にする考え方を取りますが，バイリンガル教育研究では，個人のもつさまざまな言語資源を総体としてとらえます．つまり，日本に暮らす英語のネィティブスピーカーと英語で話している場合，あなたの英語が通じなかったら相手の日本語力も活用して，コミュニケーションが成立すればそれでよい．また，複数言語話者が3人か4人いたら，さまざまな言語の組合せでやり取りをしながら全員のコミュニケーションをはかれるなら，それでよい，という視点でコミュニケーションの成否をとらえるのです．

　英語が世界の共通言語として広く使われるようになった現在では，異なる言語を母語とする人たちがさまざまな環境のもと世界中で英語を学んでいます．このため，バイリンガル教育研究の中でも，2番目の習得言語として英語を目標にする研究は最も歴史も長く，またさまざまな文脈で行われてきています．こうした研究を参照することは，私たちが英語を学ぶ上で考えるべきことについて，新たな視点をもたらしてくれるのです．

研究の大切さ

バイリンガル教育研究は，バイリンガル・マルチリンガルの学習者を対象として扱います．とりわけ研究の中心になるのは，学齢期を複数言語環境ですごす子どもたちの成長についてです．こうした子どもたちの言語発達については，何か普通でない，または望ましくないあり方とみなす傾向が一般社会にはみられます．「小さいうちから2つの言語に接すると混乱する」とか，「どちらの言語も中途半端になってしまう」などの言説は非常に大きな影響力をもっています．モノリンガルこそが「普通」であるとみなす傾向が強い社会の中で，周縁部分に追いやられてしまいがちなこうした子どもたちに光を当て，その子たちが輝けるような教育のあり方を考えることがバイリンガル教育研究のめざすところです．そのため，バイリンガル教育研究は社会正義という概念と深いつながりをもっています．社会的に力を奪われてきた人々に力を与えるための，Empowerment としての教育という教育観がその根底にあります．

さまざまな社会的文脈の中でつくり上げられた規範意識に閉じ込められて苦しむ学習者や，彼らに寄り添う親・教師たちの実践を肯定的に受け止め，その価値に光を当てながらよりよい教育のあり方を模索していくこと，そしてそれによってよりよい社会のあり方を考えていくところにバイリンガル教育研究の面白さと意義があると思います．

この章のトピック

バイリンガル教育研究の紹介，という目的のため，この章ではまずバイリンガル教育研究分野で著名な研究者の理論を概観します．社会に根強くはびこる，「モノリンガル的なバイリンガルのとらえ方」の問題点について理解し，バイリンガルのもつ言語資源を総体としてとらえることの重要性について理解することがバイリンガル教育研究の基盤となります．続いてこの章では，バイリンガル教育研究の多面性について目を向けます．バイリンガル教育について考える上では，個人のアイデンティティや家族のあり方などミクロな視点と，個人を取り巻く社会的政治的な環境というマクロな視点の両方が重要になります．

バイリンガル教育研究を概観した後，こうした研究が日本の英語教育に与える示唆について考えます．「英語学習者」として生徒を見るのではなく，「萌芽的バイリンガル」としてみることで日本の英語教育はどのように変わるのでしょうか．また，教師自身を「非ネィティブの英語教師」または「ネィティブの英語教師」

として見るのではなく，さまざまなレベルのバイリンガルの教師であるととらえることで教師自身の立ち位置や，教師同士の関係性はどのように変わっていくでしょうか．バイリンガル教育の視点を取り入れることで日本の英語教育がどのように変わるか一緒に考えてみましょう．

研究の素材

　バイリンガル教育研究は，複数言語環境に生きる人々の言語使用と社会の関係や，言語教育や移民などの政策と言語使用の関係についての研究，複数言語の習得にはどんな教育が効果的なのかといった研究など，多様な課題を扱う学際的な分野です．そのため，扱うデータのタイプもその分析方法もきわめて多岐にわたります．

　教育効果の検証というテーマについては，教育的介入の前後で特定の言語運用能力がどの程度伸びたのか，数量的に計測し，統計的に分析・解釈するという量的研究が多く行われています．こうした手法での研究を行う場合には，測りたいものをどのように測るのか，というコンストラクト（構成概念）の策定が重要になります．例えば，第二言語での作文指導においてある教育的介入の効果を確認しようとする場合，何をもって「作文力が伸びた」とみなすのか，ということが問題になるわけです．たくさんの英単語を使って長い作文を書けばより優れた作文とみなすのか，より洗練された語を使って書いた作文がよりよい作文なのか，それとも明確な構成がある作文がより優れた作文なのか，ということです．作文の優劣をどのように設定し，さらにそれをどう測定するのか，ということを決めるのが研究デザインの重要な部分になりますし，研究を行う上で一番ワクワクする部分でもあります．こうした教育的介入の効果の検証だけではなく，教育現場に行って授業の様子を観察する場合もありますし，学習者の発話や作文などの言語データを集めて，その特徴をさまざまな観点から分析することもあります．

　研究課題がバイリンガルな個人に向けられている場合は，アンケート用紙を用いた量的研究を行ったり，インタビュー調査を行って質的に分析したりすることもあります．社会学から手法を借り，エスノグラフィー[1]を行うこともあります．質的研究においては，「研究者が見たいものを見たいように分析してみせているだけ」という批判に耐えられるよう，分析の手続きを透明化し，明確に提示する

1　参与観察やフィールドワークなどを通じて行う質的な調査．そのコンテクストにおけるさまざまな事象をつぶさに観察・記録することから始まり，研究課題は研究の深まりと同時に生成されていく．

ための工夫が求められます．個人のアイデンティティに深く関わる言語使用についてのインタビューは，インタビュアーとインタビュイーの深い信頼関係の上に成り立つものですから，常に研究倫理について考え，「なぜ，研究するのか」「誰のために研究するのか」と自省しながら考察を深めていく必要があります．

研究がめざすこと

　人間にとって，言葉とは，他者とつながるためのコミュニケーションに必要不可欠なものです．同時に，言葉は，思考を深める上できわめて重要なツールでもあります．このため，言葉は個人のアイデンティティに深く関わり，親子関係や社会関係の構築の上でも重要な役割を果たすのです．

　世界全体でみれば，複数言語を日常的に使う人の数はモノリンガルの数をはるかにしのぐとされています．にもかかわらず教育の現場では，モノリンガルの言語使用が規範とされることがまだまだ多く，そうした教育現場ではバイリンガル・マルチリンガルの子どもたちの言語資源が十分に活用されないまま，顧みられずにいるのです．バイリンガル教育研究は，そうした子どもたちの言語資源を総体としてとらえ，それらを存分に活用しながら子どもたちの学びを深めていくことをめざします．バイリンガル教育について考えることは，多様な言語資源が共存する社会について考えることと直結していますし，思考およびコミュニケーションの本質とは何か，という問いにも直結しています．さまざまに異なる人々が互いの違いを認め，そうした違いに敬意を払いつつ共存をめざすこのアプローチは，現代において，私たちが進むべき道筋を示す道しるべの役割を果たしていると言えるのではないでしょうか．

Teaching English in Japan with a Bilingual Education Perspective

TABLE OF CONTENTS

1. Introduction

Castles et al. (2014) illustrate how migration has gained political salience in recent years, calling the 21st century 'the age of migration'. Although no one can foresee the impact of COVID-19 on globalisation, it is inconceivable that the demand for education in bi/multilingual contexts will decrease. This is because the majority of the world's population are already bi/multilingual; Baker and Wright (2017) estimate that 'between half and two-thirds of the world's population is bilingual to some degree' (p. 9). However, the vast majority of classrooms across the globe are constrained by monolingual bias, and do not accommodate the needs of the children growing up in the multilingual world. This paper aims to offer an introduction to bilingual education research and to discuss its relevance to English education in Japan. First, the concept of bilingualism is explored, with an introduction to the prominent frameworks in the field, followed by a discussion of the multifacetedness of this discipline, that is how bilingualism needs to be considered both at individual levels and socio-political levels. The pedagogical implications we can draw from bilingual education research relevant to English teaching in Japan will be discussed to conclude the chapter.

2. Bilinguals: Not the Sum of Two Monolinguals

Defining *bilingualism* is not as straightforward as it may seem. The popular image of a 'bilingual' might be someone who has high competencies, or native-like abilities, in two languages. Such an image of 'balanced bilinguals' has been influential as the idealised model of bilingualism.

Despite its prevalence among public figures and policymakers, educators, and even bilinguals themselves, the view that sees bilinguals as 'two separate monolinguals in one person' (Grosjean, 1989, p. 5) has been rigorously criticised by many researchers. Grosjean (1989), calling such a view 'the monolingual (or fractional) view of bilingualism', points out that by the notions of 'balanced' or 'true' bilinguals, almost all bilinguals are being stigmatised as being 'not true' bilinguals. Bilingual children are often viewed as incompetent, because they are assessed using the same criteria as monolingual native speakers. Stigmatising bilinguals as incompetent becomes especially apparent when bilinguals switch languages. Very often bilinguals are denied the use of both their languages in their educational settings in the belief that maximising the exposure to the target language accelerates language acquisi-

Figure 1 *The 'Dual-Iceberg' Representation of Bilingual Proficiency*
［Cummins, 1980/2001, p. 118］

tion—an assumption supported by no research evidence.

Another negative consequence of the monolingual view of bilinguals is that bilinguals are viewed as being exceptional rather than the norm, leading to negative assumptions about the cognitive development of bilinguals. Take, for example, the heated debate that took place before introducing English teaching at the elementary level in Japan. Some of the strongest opposition came from educators arguing that early introduction of a foreign language can hinder students' linguistic as well as cognitive development (e.g., Otsu, 2009). Again, such an assumption has no scientific basis, especially since bi/multilinguals outnumber monolinguals in the world.

In order to avoid the pitfalls of the monolingual view of bilingualism, Grosjean (2012) suggests defining bilinguals by their use of two (or more) languages and offers a definition of bilinguals as *'those who use two or more languages (or dialects) in their everyday lives'* (p. 4, emphasis in original). Focusing on use rather than proficiency will help define bilinguals broadly enough to legitimately include what García (2009) calls 'emergent bilinguals', but not so broad as to include almost everyone in the world who has contact with more than one language.

Grosjean's criticism of monolingual views of bilingualism is fully compatible with other researchers. Cummins is one of the most influential of such researchers, whose *Linguistic Interdependence Hypothesis* and the dual iceberg model that presents a visual image (Figure 1) of his hypothesis has been the cornerstone of bilingual education research. Cummins (1980/2001) proposed the existence of a *common underlying proficiency* in the linguistic abilities of bilinguals, which supports the development of the two languages equally.

This hypothesis was proposed to refute the common belief in the *maximum exposure hypothesis* (Cummins, 2001), or the belief that a child's second language (hereafter L2) acquisition is achieved fastest when the child is exposed to that language longest. Many policymakers and educators, based on such a belief, suggest that the parents of culturally and linguistically diverse (hereafter CLD) children use L2 even at home if possible and minimise the child's exposure to the heritage language[2] (hereafter HL). However, much research evidence has been presented to show how developing HL can actually help children succeed academically (e.g. Thomas and Collier, 1997).

Cummins' notion of a common underlying proficiency is especially important from a pedagogical point of view. If one accepts that learning is built on the bedrock of the knowledge that people already possess, then activating the knowledge and skills acquired in their first language (hereafter L1) in teaching CLD students becomes vital. That is why the proponents of bilingual education such as García (2009) support translanguaging, or the use of any linguistic repertoire that a CLD student can bring to his/her learning.[3] By legitimatising the use of their L1 as well as their L2 in their learning, educators can give more autonomy in learning to the student themselves.

3. The Individual, Social, and Political Aspects of Bilingual Education

I will now turn the reader's attention to the multifacetedness of bilingualism and bilingual education—that is, how it relates to people both at the individual level and at socio-political levels.

Language is inextricably intertwined with individuals' sense of identity (Miyazaki, 2014), because many think of language as the foundation of culture and the bond that connects people 'of their kind'. When asked why they

---

2   Heritage language refers to a language that differs from the majority language used in the society but is the language used by one or both of the parents of the speaker. It can be, though is not necessarily, used at home, leading to diverse educational needs of speakers. Heritage languages speakers are known to have types of motivation that are distinct from those of foreign language or second language learners because of their strong associations with the speakers' identity.

3   The same argument applies to education for deaf children. All of the researchers cited in this section strongly advocate the use of sign language in deaf education, a practice not widely implemented in many schools for the deaf across the world.

want their children to learn the language they speak, many parents express their wish to share their identity and their roots (Sano, 2020). For many HL learners, maintaining their HL is a heavy burden, but failing to do so often leaves a sense of guilt, and that is where learning an HL differs from learning a foreign language.

Sometimes, learning one's HL is judged socially. HL learners can feel stigmatised for being a speaker of a minority language. The degree of such stigmatisation is stronger with languages that are socially less valued as 'useful', or in the words of Landry and Allard (1991), those with less ethno-linguistic vitality.[4] Many HL speakers internalise such a stigma and go through a phase when they hide their ability to speak/understand the language, in order to blend into the host society. Cummins (2001), emphasising the important role of educators in reversing the 'coercive relations of power', claims:

> [C] ulturally diverse students are disempowered educationally in very much the same way that their communities have been disempowered historically in their interactions with societal institutions. ... In other words, a genuine commitment to helping all students succeed academically requires a willingness on the part of educators, individually and collectively, to challenge aspects of the power structure in the wider society. (p. vii)

HL learners of more socially 'valued' languages are not free from social pressure, either, but are pressured to have a high command of that language (Sano, 2018). Despite the naïve belief that growing up in a bilingual family automatically guarantees one to become bilingual, CLDs do not become bilinguals effortlessly, and many struggle to achieve the high competencies needed to avoid a stigma for wasting their privileges.

As shown above, language and language education have tremendous meaning for individuals and are influenced by the surrounding society. De-

---

4   Ethnographic vitality is a concept that includes the following four aspects: demographic capital (the size of the population of speakers of the language in question), political capital (how politically influential the community is), economic capital (how economically influential the community is), and cultural capital (how widely appreciated their culture is in society). These four aspects influence the positive or negative attitudes of society as a whole towards the linguistic minority community.

bates about language and language education are also highly political by nature. Very often linguistic minorities are viewed as 'threats' to the dominant culture of the nation, because people accept that language is inextricably intertwined with culture. If someone does not speak 'your' language, it is thought that he/she will not share the cultural values that you have, and therefore will stay 'foreign' to you, or will seem '"the enemy within"—a threat to nationhood' (Cummins, 2001, p. ix). Such a xenophobic tendency is not unique to Japan but has been reported in many countries with hegemonic languages. Blackledge and Creese (2010) explain how the general view on multilingualism both forms and is formed by political debates in the British context as follows, but their statement applies to many countries around the globe:

> As these political arguments become naturalised, they make their way into debates about education policy and practice, and may be further accepted as natural. A common-sense view emerges, and appears to be accepted, that the use, teaching and learning of minority languages in schools in England constitutes not only a threat to children's educational attainment, but a threat to society in general. (p. 10)

Despite the intuitive appeal of such a negative view of bilingual education to many laypeople, research evidence leads us to the completely opposite conclusion. Helping CLD children maintain and develop their HL does not hinder their educational success in their second language, but supports it, because learning takes place based on existing knowledge. Hornberger (2005) argues:

> [B] i/multilinguals' learning is maximized when they are allowed and enabled to draw from across all their existing language skills (in two+ languages), rather than being constrained and inhibited from doing so by monolingual instructional assumptions and practices (p. 607).

Cummins (2008), in concert with Hornberger, makes a strong case for 'teaching for transfer', where teachers encourage students to make active use of their existing knowledge acquired through their L1 to deepen their learning in their L2. It is not only a matter of activating schemata, however. It is a way of affirming the identities of CLD students, by establishing mutual respect and trust between the teachers and the students. As Cummins (2001) emphasises, '[r]espect and trust imply that educators listen carefully to their students' perspectives and learn from their students. If teachers are not learning much from their students, it is probable that their students are not learning much from them' (p. 4).

Let us now turn to the final thesis of this essay, how bilingual education research can help us think about education in general, and language education in particular, in the Japanese context.

4.　Pedagogical Implications for English Education in Japan

As previous sections illustrated, the respect for the entire linguistic repertoire that students bring into classrooms is the core concept of bilingual education, and such a view has several important implications for English teaching in Japan.

One of the biggest implications is that teachers are required to shift their view of students from 'English language learners' to 'emergent bilinguals', which has at least two consequences. One is a change in the focus of assessment. When viewing students as English language learners, teachers assess their achievement against the native speaker norm, and the emphasis is on error correction. By viewing students as emergent bilinguals, the focus of evaluation shifts to what contributions they can make to the multilingual world as bilingual speakers. To take full advantage of being bilinguals/multilinguals requires learners to make active use of their entire linguistic repertoires, including their first languages.

The other welcome consequence of the shift in teachers' view of students relates to the use of students' L1 in the classroom. This change is particularly important to CLDs, whose presence is becoming increasingly apparent in Japanese classrooms. It is crucial that English teachers acknowledge the varying needs of CLD students in learning English, especially when some of them may come from a country that uses English as an official language. There have been many cases where English teachers in Japan view the varieties of Englishes outside of the Inner Circle in Kachru's model as inauthentic or inaccurate (refer to Chapter 1 of this book for the related discussion). English teachers should be particularly careful to respect various types of Englishes.

Making use of students' L1 in classrooms is equally important when it is not English. If the L1 is a language that has many cognates to English, such as Spanish or Portuguese, for example, it is vital to make explicit use of it. Even when their L1 is typologically far apart from English, the fact that students are already bilinguals makes qualitative differences in language acquisition (Bialystok & Barac, 2012). Teachers should cultivate the metalinguistic abilities that bilingual students possess in acquiring the third language.

Encouraging students to make use of their L1 in learning English also applies to Japanese students. While the policy of using English as much as possible should be promoted in terms of maximising the students' exposure to the target language, teachers should be cautious with such a policy, because it can exclude students with lesser proficiency from actively participating in the class. What is called for, then, is the strategic use of the stronger language to enhance the learning of the weaker language; a pedagogical approach known as translanguaging (García, 2009). One important point to be made here is that translanguaging is not a celebration of the chaotic blending of two or more languages. García, Johnson, and Seltzer (2017) explain this focus on teachers' intentionality as follows:

> Teachers in translanguaging classrooms embrace a flexible stance toward students' dynamic bilingualism. This does not mean that they do away with objectives and goals for students' language practices. On the contrary, teachers of bilingual students always think strategically about how they use language (p. 56).

Also, fostering bilingual/multilingual identities in Japanese speakers is equally important. When speaking an L2 as a non-native speaker (NNS), people often feel a sense of shame or even guilt in a moment of communication breakdown. Such negative feelings evaporate when one has a strong positive identity as a bilingual speaker. The focus is on what they can contribute to the world via their L2. In helping students foster such bilingual identities, teachers need to intentionally orient the students to take advantage of being bilinguals to the full extent.

The paradigm shift from 'English education' to 'Bilingual education' changes not only how students are viewed by the teachers but how teachers view themselves, as well. When viewing English education from a monolingual perspective, the criteria of good teachers will be solely on proficiency in

English, and then the best candidates will always be the native speakers. In this view, the roles of Japanese teachers will be limited to explaining grammatical points and to translating what the native speaker (NS) teacher says when necessary. However, if both NS teachers and NNS teachers are viewed as bilingual teachers at differing points of the bilingual continuum, teachers can act as role models of language learners for the students; they can share learning strategies that worked best for them with their students, as well as set a great example of working together in a multilingual environment via collaboration.

5. Conclusion

As has been shown in this essay, researching bilingual education forces educators to re-think what education really is, and what role language plays in education. If we accept the Vygotskian view of language as the most important tool people make use of in thinking, language deserves a special status in education because it is the foundation of cognitive development. Without language, one cannot access new knowledge, nor can one develop thoughts. Therefore, it is vital for teachers to legitimatise the use of the linguistic tools that students possess. Language also deserves a special status in education because it can be viewed as linguistic capital in Bourdieu's sense. (See García 2009, p. 12). The bilingual approach to education respects every linguistic resource that students bring to the classroom as legitimate and valuable. The objectives of bilingual education are to educate generally, meaningfully, equitably, and for tolerance and appreciation of diversity. These objectives will guide English education in Japan, too.

▌ References

Baker, C., & Wright, W. E. (2017). *Foundations of bilingual education and bilingualism* (6th edition). Multilingual Matters.

Bialystok, E., & Barac, R. (2012). Emerging bilingualism: Dissociating advantages for metalinguistic awareness and executive control. *Cognition, 122* (1), 67-73.

Blackledge, A., & Creese, A. (2010). *Multilingualism: A critical perspective.* Continuum International Publishing Group.

Castles, S., de Haas, H., & Miller, M. J. (2014). *The age of migration: International population movements in the modern world.* (Fifth edition). Palgrave Macmillan.

Cummins, J. (1980/2001). The entry and exit fallacy in bilingual education. In C. Baker and N. Hornberger (Eds.), *An introductory reader to the writings of Jim Cummins* (pp. 110-138). Multilingual Matters.

Cummins, J. (2000). *Language, power and pedagogy: Bilingual children in the crossfire*. Multilingual Matters.

Cummins, J. (2001). *Negotiating identities: Education for empowerment in a diverse society* (2nd Ed.). California Association for Bilingual Education.

Cummins, J. (2008). Teaching for transfer: Challenging the two solitudes assumption in bilingual education. In J. Cummins and N. H. Hornberger (Eds.), *Encyclopedia of language and education, Volume 5* (pp. 65-75). Springer.

García, O. (2009). *Bilingual education in the 21st century: A global perspective*. Wiley-Blackwell.

García, O., Johnson, S. I., & Seltzer, K. (2017). *The translanguaging classroom: Leveraging student bilingualism for learning*. Caslon.

Grosjean, F. (1989). Neurolinguists, beware! The bilingual is not two monolinguals in one person. *Brain and Language, 36*, 3-15.

Grosjean, F. (2012). *Bilingual: Life and reality* (Reprint ed.). Harvard University Press.

Hornberger, N. (2005). Opening and filling up implementation and ideological spaces in heritage language education. *The Modern Language Journal, 89*, 605-609.

Landry, R., & Allard, R. (1991). Can schools promote additive bilingualism in minority group children? In L. Malavé & G. Duquette (Eds.), *Language, culture, and cognition: A collection of studies in first and second language acquisition* (pp. 198-231). Multilingual Matters.

Sano, A. (2020). Successful family language policy in fostering children's biliteracy: Focusing on the parents of heritage language speakers in the U. K. *BATJ Journal, 21*, 4-21.

Thomas, W. P. & Collier, V. (1997). *School effectiveness for language minority students*. National Clearinghouse for Bilingual Education.

大津由紀雄 (2009) 『危機に立つ日本の英語教育』慶應義塾大学出版会.

佐野愛子 (2018)「複数言語社会香港における継承日本語学習者の多様な言語学習環境」研究代表者 河合靖『東アジア圏の複言語主義共同体の構築―多言語社会香港からの示唆―』平成 27 年～平成 29 年度 科学研究費補助金 基

盤研究（B）（一般）（課題番号：15H03221）研究成果報告書 pp.98-124.
(http://translanguaging.sakura.ne.jp/hkp48/wp-content/
uploads/2018/03/03-kobayashi_sano_yorozu.pdf).
宮崎幸江編（2014）『日本に住む多文化の子どもと教育―ことばと文化のはざま
で生きる』上智大学出版.

▌ Further Reading

Cummins, J. (2001). *Negotiating identities: Education for empowerment in a diverse society.* (Second edition). California Association for Bilingual Education.

García, O., Johnson, S. I., & Seltzer, K. (2017). *The translanguaging classroom: Leveraging student bilingualism for learning.* Caslon.

▌ 日本語文献案内

　日本語でバイリンガル教育研究の概説をしたものに，中島（2016）があります．また，この章で紹介したジム・カミンズ博士の理論のうち最も重要な5つの論文をまとめたものもありますので，是非参考にしてみてください．

中島和子『バイリンガル教育の方法：12歳までに親と教師ができること』完全改訂版，アルク，2016年.
ジム・カミンズ／中島和子著訳『言語マイノリティを支える教育』新装版，明石書店，2021年.

▌ 考えてみよう

1.　これまであなたが受けてきた英語の授業を思い出してください．その教室にフィリピン出身の生徒がいたとしたら，どのような支援を教師はできる／すべきでしょうか．また，ブラジル出身の生徒がいた場合，中国出身の生徒がいた場合はどうでしょうか．

2.　上記のような授業を行った場合，それは日本語を母語とするマジョリティの生徒たちにはどのような効果があるでしょうか．

佐野　愛子
Aiko SANO

言語, アイデンティティ, テクノロジー

Language, Identities, and Technology

概要

　この章では，テクノロジーの使用が言語とアイデンティティの形成に与える影響について考察します．テクノロジーと言語には長い歴史があり，個人の自己認識（アイデンティティ）にも関係があります．人がコミュニケーションをとり，意味交渉するときに，自己の共同構築（co-construction of self）が自然に起こります．スマートフォンやパソコンなどの情報機器伝達ツールの違いによって，コミュニケーションはどのような影響を受けるのでしょうか．自己の共同構築にテクノロジーと言語はどのように相互作用しているのでしょうか．電話やテレビ，そしてインターネットなどのさまざまなメディアが生活に加わり，他者との関係の中で構築される自己イメージは，サイバースペースのテクノロジー，特にソーシャルメディアの影響を強く受けるようになりました．これらの影響に関する研究を紹介します．

図1　この章で使用されている単語から生成されたワードクラウド．ワードクラウドは，コミュニケーションメディアで使用される単語の頻度を視覚化する方法の1つである

国際英語文化の中の, 言語・アイデンティティ・テクノロジーについての研究

　言語, アイデンティティ, テクノロジーの関連性を, 国際英語文化という大きな分野で研究する最も重要な理由は, テクノロジー（特にインターネット）が, 私たちをより大きく, グローバルな言語ユーザーのコミュニティに結びつけているからです. 20世紀の言語は, ラジオ, 電話, 映画, テレビなどのメディアに強い影響を受けています. このようなメディアのおかげで, さまざまな文化圏の人々がこれまで以上に遠く離れた場所に居ながらアイデアや情報を交換できるようになりました. 21世紀には, インターネットのユビキタス性[1]により, 世界のどこにいても, いつでも, 誰からでも, 文字通り手のひらの上であらゆる情報を得ることができます. ますます多くの情報にアクセスできるようになったことで, 言語交換量は飛躍的に増加しました. しかし, このように情報, アイデア, 言語のやり取りがどんどん増えていくことは, 誤った情報の流れが増えていくという暗黒面をももたらします. オンラインで, 文字だけではなくインタラクティブな画像やビデオを使用することで, きわめて説得力のある方法で実在しない人物のふりをすることができるようになりました. また, 世界中の人々からのフィードバックが, オンラインでの自分自身の見方や見せ方に影響を与えることもあります. 研究は, こうした状況下での英語によるコミュニケーション文化について, 多くを教えてくれます.

研究の楽しさ

　言語とアイデンティティとテクノロジーについて研究することの面白さは, この研究が英語学や異文化コミュニケーション学のほぼすべての側面, そしてほとんどすべての人の日常生活に密接に関係している点です.

　あなたが朝起きて, 最初にすることは何ですか. テレビをつけて, 朝のニュースを見ますか. 朝刊を読みますか. あるいはスマートフォンをオンにして, 寝ている間にSNSで何が起こったかを確認しますか（おそらくこの可能性が最も高いでしょう）. 日常的にテクノロジーと接する中, テクノロジーはあなた自身の一部になっています. テクノロジーを使わない自分を想像できますか.

　言葉の使い方とテクノロジーの関係を研究することは, 人間としての私たちを理解するためのヒントになります. 例えば, どの画像をSNS上で使用すれば,

---

1　いつでもどこでも利用できるという性質.

それは自分が自身をどう見ているか，あるいは他人にどう見られたいと思っているかについて，何かしらのメッセージを示すことにもなります．インターネットの重要性が増し，人間の活動のほぼすべての側面と切り離せなくなっている中（Internet of Things「モノのインターネット」），テクノロジーと人間性の相互作用を調べることは重要です．オンラインでビデオを見たり，友人とメールをしたりすることは楽しい活動であるべきで，そのためにもテクノロジーは，人間性に逆らわない方向で利用されねばなりません．

この章のトピック

　本章ではまず，言語はテクノロジーの生みの親であると同時にその産物でもあるという考え方を紹介し，言語とテクノロジーの相互作用が自己の共同構築に与える影響を説明します．音を表すために文字記号を使用した当初から，言語とテクノロジーは互いに結びついていました．文字を書くことで言語を初めて記録することができ，音，言葉，アイデア，思考，感情，イメージを未来へ引き継ぐことができるようになりました．この基本的な技術が，自然界のさまざまな素材を使って後にどのように発展したかを確認し，「テクノロジー」が機械的または電子的な性質をもつものだけを指すという認識を改めます．

　次に，自己の共同構築のプロセスを考えます．共同構築は，さまざまな社会的文脈の中で，さまざまな対話者とさまざまな方法で使用される言葉やフレーズの交換を通して行われます．オンライン会議では，画像やビデオフィルター，バーチャルな背景などが使用できます．これらはオンライン会議で使用される言語にどのような影響を与えているでしょうか．本章の最後に，偽の画像や動画，誤解を招くプロフィールはどのような問題を引き起こしているのか，関連する問題点を検討します．

研究の素材

　言語や技術を研究するための資料にはさまざまな種類があり，その分析方法も多様です．最も基本的な言語資料は，電話インタビュー，テレビ放送，映画のセリフ，インターネットのストリーミングサイト上のビデオなど，実際に使用された言語を書き起こしたものです．一般に販売される学習教材にあるコミュニケーションの例を挙げると，特定の使用者を想定してつくられ，その分野の基準に合わせて意図的に演じられているため，必ずしも本物のテキストとは言えません．

より現実に近い言語資料は，SNS で簡単に入手できます．特に Twitter や Facebook などの人気サイトは，誰でも無料で利用できます．キーワードを検索するだけで，特定のトピックについてどのような言葉が使われているかを知ることができます．もちろん，データを収集する最も簡単な方法は，会話の音声やビデオを記録し，話した言葉を書き写すことです．ここでも，オンライン会議や自動文字起こしなどの最新技術が活躍します．

　さまざまなテクノロジーを使った言語コミュニケーション（特に，オンラインでのチャット，SNS を使った書面での意見交換など）の言語分析には，いくつかの方法があります．最も基本的な分析は記述統計で，会話（口頭または書面）の中の単語数，文の長さ，交代回数などのテキストの特徴を数値化します．アイデアや感情を伝えるために使われるイメージに関連して，言語を分析することもできます．これは「比喩分析」と呼ばれ，特定の地域，文化，性別，階層内の役割，さらには時代によって，人々の表現方法がどのように異なるかを比較するのに役立ちます．また，「コーディング分析」では，特定の文脈や状況において，どの単語やフレーズがより頻繁に使用されているかを調べます．

　言語，アイデンティティ，テクノロジーの研究分野では，非言語のコミュニケーション形態を研究素材とすることで，言語とコミュニケーションについての理解を深めることができます．例えば，オンラインでの議論に使われる画像が，個人のパーソナリティの側面をどのように反映し，矛盾したり，構築したりするのかが観察できます．絵文字のような画像を調べれば，文化的な違いを明らかにすることもできます．アバター（オンラインユーザーが自分を表現するために選んだ画像）を比較・分析すると，個人の自己意識がテクノロジーの利用によって変化する様子を知ることもできます．

　最後に，遠隔会議ソフトウェアは，オンラインでのビデオ会話を記録し，書き起こすことができます．ジェスチャー，顔の表情，その他の非言語的なコミュニケーションの形態を調査できます．このようなソフトウェアを用いて，参加者はテキストチャットや電子ファイルを送受信することができます．そのため，情報を送受信する者について，対面でのコミュニケーションとは大きく異なるイメージを与えることができます．こうしたものも，研究素材となります．

研究がめざすこと

　言語とテクノロジーの相互作用に関する研究では，テクノロジーの使用が言語に与える影響とその変化を理解するだけでなく，個人のアイデンティティがどのように表現され，変化し，描かれ，認識されるのかを解明しようとします．これ

は学際的な分野です．社会学，心理学，言語学，そして技術的・専門的なコミュニケーションのリソースや概念を活用し，言語の使用者が総合的なコミュニケーションスキルを向上させるだけでなく，異文化間の認識や心理的な幸福感を高める方法の解明をめざしています．インターネットは現代社会のほぼすべての側面と絡み合っているため，インターネットが言語使用にどのような影響を与えるかを研究することは，もともと異なる文化的背景をもち，現在はグローバルなインターネットコミュニティの中でオンラインアイデンティティをもつ人々の言葉をどのように解釈すべきかを教えてくれます．また，スマートフォンやさまざまなソーシャルメディア・アプリの使用に伴って生じるアイデンティティ，いわゆる「ポータブル・アイデンティティ」の研究も，私たちが何者であり，何者になるのか，そしてそれが将来のコミュニケーションにどのような影響を与えるのかを理解する上で重要です．

　「トロイのヘレネーは千隻の船を推進させた顔」と言われ，トロイア戦争が勃発したことは有名です．21 世紀の今，「1000 発のミサイルを発射するツイート」と言われるほど，テクノロジーの誤用やその機能と役割に関する誤解が，危険な状況を招く可能性は十分にあります．言語，アイデンティティ，テクノロジーに関する研究は，他者がどのように考え，感じ，私たちの言語使用や文化をどのように認識しているかを理解するのに役立ちます．これらの相互作用を理解することで，誤解やミスコミュニケーションを回避し，文化的紛争を未然に防ぐことができるかもしれません．

Language, Identities, and Technology

TABLE OF CONTENTS

1.　Introduction

Human beings communicate with each other every day in person. When they need to communicate long distance, they need technology such as a telephone, smartphone, or personal computer. However, the use of technology to communicate has a long history that reaches back thousands of years and has been essential not only to language development but also to identity formation. The interaction of technology with language and identity has been a main research topic in media and communication studies, which arose as study fields after the start of the Information Age in the mid-20th century; this interaction is increasingly important to life in the digital age of the "Internet of Things." This chapter will describe how technology use has influenced language, and how both technology and language continue to shape individuals' sense of self.

2.　A Brief History of the Technology of Language

As an aspect of daily life at home, at school, at work, and in any other social situation in which people meet and do activities with others, language is one the most fundamental intellectual tools of human beings. Language is a means of asking others for help or for offering advice to others, and thus language mediates human action. Historically, there have been many ways in which technology has enhanced language use. The very symbols used to graphically depict the sounds used to communicate are a kind of technology. This means that a hieroglyphic, alphabetic, or logographic system of writing is the original *linguistic technology*. Communication, which once was limited to spoken forms between people who were physically present, can now be preserved for people in the future or who live physically far apart.

The invention of writing coded the original message in symbols that others could understand, but the written symbols themselves can sometimes be interpreted to mean something other than the original intended message. The material technology with which the message is preserved also affects the communication. Hieroglyphs and cuneiform were symbols of language cut into soft mud bricks that later hardened. We can still read these ancient symbols thousands of years after they were first formed. Other materials such as wood, bone, and turtle shells have also been used, but historically the most commonly used *print technologies* are papyrus (made from grassy plants), parchment (made from animal skins), and paper (made from trees).

Technologies have thus affected language for millennia, ever since people first wrote their ideas in symbolic form (Figure 1). The job of writing in many societies fell to scribes, who were usually trained to read and write in religious institutions. The inventions of the printing press and moveable type allowed for greater distribution of printed materials and coincided with greater

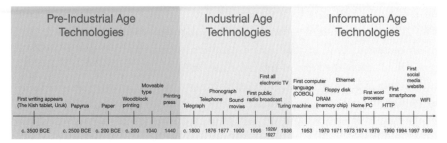

Figure 1 A timeline of technologies that affected language usage around the world. [*Note.* The timeline presented here is not to scale.]

numbers of learning facilities. As more and more people learned to read and to write, their languages came in contact, which in turn helped to create new words, grammars, and expressions.

As part of the Industrial Revolution in Europe and North America, electrical and electronic tools for language use first came into being. The telegraph allowed messages to be transmitted on wires over long distances via coded mechanical taps generating an electric impulse. Telegraph wires were later replaced by telephone wires, which transmitted the electromagnetic waves generated by human speech. Later, radio broadcasts enabled the transmission of human voice wirelessly. Edison's phonograph was the first technology that could record and replay human voice. This technology was soon followed by film, which first recorded silent images before adding voice. Television was invented before World War II, which delayed its development, but rapidly became a force in shaping language use from the late 1940s. By the mid- to late-20th century, the rise of the personal computer (PC), the Internet, and the change from analog to digital information was dramatically affecting the way in which language was created and communicated.

The Internet Age as it exists in the 21st century is just one stage in the development of language and technology. However, the introduction of mobile devices such as smartphones and tablet computers has meant not only an increase in information exchange but also a change in the very way people see themselves and others. Personal identity is directly affected by both language use and technology use. The connection between language and identity will be discussed in the next section, and how the use of technology affects both will be the focus of the section following that.

3.　How Language and Identity Are Co-created

Everyone has a *self-image* that they want others to see, and this sense of self is projected to those around them both verbally and physically. The way people behave, their physical appearance (e.g., hairstyle, clothing, jewelry), and the words they use contribute to the projection of a self-image as they try to influence the impression that others have of them (Goffman, 1959). For example, people may want others to see them as strong, good-looking, smart, or cool. However, other people may perceive them differently, and the image also may change depending on the social group in which the interaction occurs. The words people use to communicate additionally help to shape the way they see themselves and others. Different words and phrases are used with different groups of people. For example, people might use a certain word or phrase with friends that they wouldn't use with parents, teachers, or work colleagues. One group might perceive them as friendly and outgoing, while another might have the impression that they are reserved and quiet. The way others perceive them will then influence the language they use, so that language and identity construction inform each other. In this way, both language and identity are *negotiated* or *co-constructed* between people in a social group, and this co-construction of identity changes over time as people come to know more about one another.

The question many have recently is to what degree *long distance communication* affects the sense of self. The global COVID-19 pandemic that began in December 2019 drastically changed communication patterns around the world. Suddenly students, educators, and many business workers were forced to rely heavily on technology for communication with friends and colleagues. Even family relationships were affected, as people found themselves using teleconference software to speak with relatives instead of traveling to meet in person. This sudden change, however, was only an acceleration of a trend at universities in North America and Europe that started several years prior to the pandemic.

Since the beginning of the 21st century, many universities have encouraged online, or *e-learning*, education in which students do not physically attend any classes. Students were of course already interacting online with their peers for educational and recreational purposes in the 1990s. But a kind of distance education promoted by North American universities became known as *massively open online courses* (MOOCs), fully online courses in which hundreds, thousands, and even hundreds of thousands of students have participated (Kaplan & Haenlein, 2016). E-learning usually requires students to create an account in a *course management system* or *learning management system* (CMS or LMS), where the instructor uploads learning materials, such as digital files for reading, listening, or watching. Students interact online in various forums, collaborative blogs, and wikis, which are all monitored by a course instructor or teaching assistant. The resulting co-construction of online identities, with both positive and negative aspects, will be the focus of the next section.

4. Computers, the Internet, and You

Originally called "social networking services" (and still known as SNS in Japan), *social media* started in the mid-1990s with the appearance of interactive websites. These sites were collectively termed "Web 2.0" to distinguish them from previous static, unchanging websites whose function was simply to give information in one direction, from creator to user (Berry, 1995/2017). However, with the advent of the smartphone in 2005 and websites such as Facebook, Twitter, and YouTube that can be accessed from a smartphone application, or *app* for short, anyone can co-create websites and exchange information freely. Online interaction by literally billions of people around the world now takes place on a near-constant basis. In 2015, it was reported that teenagers in the US spent over an hour each day on social media websites and used their smartphones over six hours a day in total (Common Sense Media, 2015, p. 20). This no doubt has only increased in the past few years and particularly since early 2020.

As social interaction online increases, it is accompanied by changes in social identity. During social media interaction, people are not physically present with each other, so there is already an additional layer of perception. Each *interlocutor*, or a communication partner, has to determine whether the message they are trying to convey has been influenced by the method of the communication—the *communication medium*. In many cases, the communication medium is more important than the content of the communication, as exemplified in the famous phrase "The medium is the message" (MacLuhan, 1964). Online communication media are different from face to face (*F2F*) and simple telephone communication. Because online communication can be saved in text, audio, or video format, internet users can build up a *user profile* that gives a certain impression to other users. Some social media users choose to deliberately adopt a different *persona*, an aspect of themselves they wish others online to perceive. They may even use an *avatar*, or an image that represents this persona, to influence the impression that other people have of them online. (See *sockpuppetry* below for when this gets out of control.)

Communicating online can be done by using symbols (writing/reading), using audio/video (speaking/listening/watching), or a combination (live video-conferencing). *Computer-mediated communication* (*CMC*) can occur at the same time (synchronous) or at different times (asynchronous). However, synchronous CMC using *texting* is very different than when using audiovisual technology. Without physical gestures or facial expressions to help the other person understand the nuance, the written message can be misinterpreted. This is why texting often includes emoji (originally called "emoticons" in English), such as faces that smile, cry, look confused, or surprised. Here, too, some emoji can be interpreted differently than the intended meaning, depending on the cultural or personal background of the interlocutors (Figure 2). Using videoconferencing software can facilitate communication better than texting not only because speaking is easier than writing, but also interlocutors can see each other. Turn-taking while speaking via videoconferencing can be difficult, because when one person speaks others cannot be heard so easily. Making eye contact is also problematic, depending on the location of the computer camera.

Naturally, there are both advantages and disadvantages of CMC. The level of technology needed includes the device (smartphone, laptop or desktop

Figure 2　Emoji (originally "emoticons," a portmanteau of "emotion" and "icon") convey symbolic meanings similar to ancient hieroglyphs and can be used to clarify the intended meaning of a text message.

PC), the speed of the internet connection (dial-up, LAN, WIFI), and the software required (free or paid account). The ability to use the technology differs depending on the person. Where to use the technology is also an issue; computers at home may need to be shared with others, and the internet connection may also be shared, which may slow down or even accidentally interrupt the communication if too much video information is exchanged.

The presentation of the self online is also a concern to many. The sharing of images of the self, or *selfies*, can cause internet users to focus exclusively on physical appearance, and whether the selfie is a genuine, authentic image of the self largely depends on the person viewing it rather than the person who posted it (Nguyen & Barbour, 2017). Posting self-videos and selfies in order to get "likes" on social media such as Instagram, Snapchat, and Tik-Tok has been seen as potentially harmful to self-esteem but also as a means of creating *online communities of practice* (OCoP) or *virtual communities of practice* (VCoP; Dubé, Bourhis, & Jacob, 2005. See also Lave & Wenger, 1991). Unfortunately, networked communities can sometimes lead to egocentric, selfish, narcissistic behavior. This is termed *networked individualism*, where one person dominates a group for selfish purposes (Jenkins, Ito, & boyd, 2015). Additionally, there is always the potential for cyberbullying, even among those who have known each other for a long time.

Lastly, *online imposters* or *sockpuppets*—people who create a false identity to deceive others—have been cause for concern since the beginning of the internet. An online imposter typically pretends to an identity that they do not have in order to belong to another online community, to hide their true identity, or to act out a fantasy. A famous, early sockpuppet was a white business consultant in Ohio, U.S., who set up a user group on America Online (AOL). He claimed to be an indigenous tribal elder called Blue Snake and encouraged Native Americans to contribute to discussions of Native American rituals and customs but was quickly discovered to have created a false identity (Martin, 1995).

Other, more recent identity thefts have fooled even major media sources such as the *New York Times* and *CNN* (Seife, 1994). Such sockpuppets typically have fake email addresses, blogs, and social media accounts and are often created by someone who wants attention or sympathy from others due to personal trauma. However, other sockpuppets create false accounts to anonymously verbally abuse someone online, and still others are created for more nefarious purposes such as attempting to lure underage children to meet in person. CMC is thus a dangerous double-edged sword that can both help and harm those who use it.

5. Conclusion

Online communication in the 21st century has greatly expanded our communicative capabilities, but there are always risks involved and care must be taken to both protect and preserve identities. We live in an ever-expanding networked world, and the use of online communication will only increase. Yet, technology has always influenced both language and identity. The role of online technology in creating what we communicate and who we are is something to consider more carefully.

| References

Berry, D. (1995/2017). Social media spaces. http://www.ku24.com/~darrell/hybrid1.html

Dubé, L., Bourhis, A., & Jacob, R. (2005). The impact of structuring characteristics on the launching of virtual communities of practice. *Journal of Organizational Change Management, 18*(2), 145-166. https://doi.org/10.1108/0953481050589570

Common Sense Media. (2015). The Common Sense Census: Media use by tweens and teens. https://www.commonsensemedia.org/sites/default/files/uploads/research/census_researchreport.pdf

Goffman, E. (1959). *The presentation of self in everyday life*. Doubleday.

Jenkins, H., Ito, M., & boyd, d. (2015). *Participatory culture in a networked era: A conversation on youth, learning, commerce, and politics*. Polity Press.

Kaplan, A. M., & Haenlein, M. (2016). Higher education and the digital revolution: About MOOCs, SPOCs, social media, and the Cookie Monster. *Business Horizons, 59*(4), 441-450. https://doi.org/10.1016/j.bushor.2016.03.008

Lave, J., & Wenger, E. (1991). *Situated learning: Legitimate peripheral participation*. Cambridge University Press.

MacLuhan, M. (1964). *Understanding media: The extensions of man*. McGraw-Hill.

Martin, G. (1995, December 1). Internet Indian wars. *WIRED*. https://www.wired.com/1995/12/martin/

Nguyen, L., & Barbour, K. (2017). Selfies as expressively authentic identity performance. *First Monday, 22*(11). https://doi.org/10.5210/fm.v22i11.7745

Seife, D. (2014). *Virtual unreality: Just because the Internet told you, how do you know it's true?* Viking.

Further Reading

boyd, d. (2014). *It's complicated: The social lives of networked teens.* Yale University Press.

Kaplan, A. M., & Haenlein, M. (2010). Users of the world, unite! The challenges and opportunities of social media. *Business Horizons, 53*(1), 59–68. https://doi.org/10/1016/j.bushor.2009.09.003

日本語文献案内

石井僚他「SNS上の否定的な文脈への同調を抑制する情報モラル教育方法の検討」『日本教育工学会論文誌』43(4), 457-466, 2020 (https://doi.org/10.15077/jjet.43067).

久保昌平他「青年におけるアイデンティティ確立とSNSの利用および依存との因果関係の検討」『人間科学研究』10, 9-16, 2015 (http://doi.org/10.15027/39143).

考えてみよう

1. コミュニケーションをとるためにどのようなテクノロジーを使用していますか. そのデバイスを毎日・毎週・毎月どのくらい使用していますか. クラスメートと組んで比較しましょう.

2. オンラインでコミュニケーションをとるときと, 直接コミュニケーションをとるときでは,自分が別の人のように感じますか. オンラインでコミュニケーションを取る相手によって言葉の使い方が変わりますか. その理由は何でしょうか.

3. デジタルデバイス(スマートフォンなど)の使用をしばらくの間, 避けることを検討したことがありますか. 例えば, スマートフォンを1週間使用しなかったら, どのように感じますか.

4. ネット上でのいじめについて考えましょう. なぜオンラインで他人へのいじめが生じると思いますか. これを防ぐ方法は何でしょうか.

....

マシュー T. アップル
Matthew T. APPLE

和文索引

英文索引

●編者・執筆者紹介●

※［ ］内は執筆担当章

【編　者】

ウェルズ恵子（うぇるず・けいこ）　立命館大学文学部教授．博士（学術）．アメリカ文化・文学，歌詞や物語の比較研究，ヴァナキュラー言語文化研究，音楽関連文化研究を行う．著書に『黒人霊歌は生きている』『魂をゆさぶる歌に出会う』『多文化理解のためのアメリカ文化入門』（共著）などがある．　　　　　　　　　　　　　　　　　　　　　　　　　　　　　［3 章］

【編集ワーキンググループ】

岡本広毅（おかもと・ひろき）　立命館大学文学部准教授．博士（文学）．中世英語英文学，英語文化史，ファンタジー文化研究を行う．共編著に『いかにしてアーサー王は日本で受容されサブカルチャー界に君臨したか』『中世英語英文学研究の多様性とその展望』がある．［2 章］

薩摩真介（さつま・しんすけ）　立命館大学文学部准教授．Ph.D. (History)．近世イギリス史，アメリカ植民地時代史，大西洋史．イギリス海軍や北米・カリブ海の私掠者・海賊の歴史を中心に，海の歴史を研究．著書に *Britain and Colonial Maritime War in the Early Eighteenth Century*，『〈海賊〉の大英帝国』などがある．　　　　　　　　　　　　　［7 章］

杉村美奈（すぎむら・みな）　立命館大学文学部准教授．Ph.D. (Linguistics)．理論言語学（統語論・形態論）研究．日本語の複雑述語形成をはじめ，統語論・形態論インターフェース研究を主に行う．主な論文に Root vs. *n*: A study of Japanese light verb construction and its implications for nominal architecture などがある．　　　　　　　　　　　　　　［8 章］

佐野愛子（さの・あいこ）　立命館大学文学部教授．博士（学術）．専門は英語教育及びバイリンガル教育．海外に暮らす日本語継承語話者や国内に学ぶ文化的・言語的に多様な子どもたち，また，日本手話と日本語のバイリンガルとしてのろうの子どもたちの学びを支える研究を行う．　　　　　　　　　　　　　　　　　　　　　　　　　　　　　　　　　　　　［11 章］

【執筆者】

マイケル・ジェームズ・デービス（Michael James DAVIES）　立命館大学文学部教授．Master (Applied Linguistics)．研究テーマは，Global Englishes, English as a Lingua Franca (ELF), 内容言語統合型学習 (CLIL) である．共編著に *Educational Reform and International Baccalaureate in the Asia-Pacific* などがある．　　　　　　　　　　［1 章］

山本めゆ（やまもと・めゆ）　立命館大学文学部准教授．博士（文学）．南アフリカの人種主義，アジアからアフリカへの人の移動，アフリカとアジアの関係史を研究．著書に『「名誉白人」の百年：南アフリカのアジア系住民をめぐるエスノ‐人種ポリティクス』がある．　　［コラム］

坂下史子（さかした・ふみこ）　立命館大学文学部教授．Ph.D. (American Studies)．アフリカ系アメリカ人の歴史と文化，反リンチ運動の歴史，人種暴力をめぐる記憶の問題を研究．著書に『よくわかるアメリカの歴史』（共編著），『私たちが声を上げるとき』（共著）などがある．　　　　　　　　　　　　　　　　　　　　　　　　　　　　　　　　　　　　［4 章］

水島新太郎（みずしま・しんたろう）　立命館大学文学部准教授．博士（アメリカ研究）．アメリカの歴史やポピュラー文化を中心に，ジェンダーの視点から男性の多様性について研究．著書に『マンガでわかる男性学：ジェンダーレス時代を生きるために』がある．　　　　［5 章］

小川真和子（おがわ・まなこ） 立命館大学文学部教授．Ph.D.（American Studies）．日米，ハワイにおける海の民や女性の歴史研究を行う．著書に *Sea of Opportunity*，『海をめぐる対話　ハワイと日本』『海の民のハワイ』などがある． [6章]

久屋愛実（くや・あいみ） 立命館大学文学部准教授．Ph.D.（Comparative Philology and General Linguistics）．バリエーション理論に基づく日英語の変異・変化研究を行う．著書に *The diffusion of Western loanwords in contemporary Japanese: A variationist approach* などがある． [9章]

根本浩行（ねもと・ひろゆき） 立命館大学文学部教授．Ph.D.（Sociolinguistics）．社会文化理論を用いて異文化接触，アイデンティティ変容，ことばの混淆性を研究．主論文に The investment in managing interests and power through study abroad: Literacy and identities from a translingual perspective，主著に *The management of intercultural academic interaction: Student exchanges between Japanese and Australian universities* などがある． [10章]

マシュー T. アップル（Matthew T. APPLE） 立命館大学文学部教授．博士（英語教育）．主な研究領域は第二言語習得における動機づけ，可能自己理論，教育技術の使用．編著書に *Language learning motivation in Japan* などがある． [12章]

編　者
ウェルズ恵子
立命館大学文学部教授

多文化理解のための
国際英語文化入門

令和 4 年 12 月 25 日　発　行

編　　者　ウェルズ恵子

発 行 者　池　田　和　博

発 行 所　丸善出版株式会社
〒101-0051 東京都千代田区神田神保町二丁目 17 番
編 集： 電 話(03)3512-3264／FAX(03)3512-3272
営 業： 電 話(03)3512-3256／FAX(03)3512-3270
https://www.maruzen-publishing.co.jp

組版印刷・株式会社 日本制作センター／製本・株式会社 松岳社

ISBN 978-4-621-30786-1 C1082　　　Printed in Japan